C000001890

Katy Schutte is an improviser, writer, comedian, actor and director. She trained in Drama at the University of Hull before finding her true passion at iO Chicago, Second City Chicago and with teachers from The Annoyance Theatre, UCB and other world-class improv training schools. Katy has been a member of award-winning improv company The Maydays since their founding year in 2004. She performed in a twoprov with Rachel Blackman for over a decade, and performs in science-fiction show Project2. Katy is a Funny Women finalist and has written and starred in several acclaimed live comedy shows including *Schutte The Unromantic* and *Who Ya Gonna Call?* (the *Ghostbusters* fan-tribute musical). You can often catch her in TV commercials and nerdy comedy shows. Katy lives in London, and teaches and performs all over the world.

www.katyschutte.co.uk

www.ebook3000.com

THE IMPROVISER'S WAY

WAY

A LONGFORM WORKBOOK
BY KATY SCHUTTE

NICK HERN BOOKS
London
www.nickhernbooks.co.uk

A Nick Hern Book

The Improviser's Way first published in Great Britain in 2017. This new edition published in 2018 as a paperback original by Nick Hern Books Limited, The Glasshouse, 49a Goldhawk Road, London W12 8QP

Copyright © 2017, 2018 Katy Schutte

Katy Schutte has asserted her moral right to be identified as the author of this work

Cover design by Fred Deakin, with special thanks to Karen Lamond and Nat Hunter
Author photograph by Edward Moore

Printed and bound in Great Britain by Ashford Colour Press, Gosport, Hampshire

A CIP catalogue record for this book is available from the British Library

ISBN 978 1 84842 738 9

MIX
Paper from
responsible sources
FSC
www.fsc.org   FSC® C011748

Contents

Preface

This book contains both exercises and philosophies of improv, some of which are my own and others that I have come across and want to pass on. Even the things I imagine are my own are sometimes an adaptation or perversion of some earlier creation. I have tried to credit the origin of games and theories, but improv is largely an oral or kinaesthetic tradition and the beginning of any one thing is nebulous.

If I were Thor (yes please) these would be my sagas.

I would like to thank the many teachers, directors and mentors I have had over the years as much of this work is from or because of them. They include Charna Halpern, Susan Messing, Rich Sohn, Rebecca Sohn, Bill Arnett, Brandon Gardner, Lee White, Jay Rhoderick, Tim Sniffen, Jet Eveleth, Eliza Skinner, Shad Kunkle, Dylan Emery, Alan Marriott, Chris Johnston, Nancy Howland Walker, Joe Bill, John Cremer, Marshall Stern, Alex Fendrich, Brian Posen, Mary Scruggs, Bina Martin, Claudia Wallace, Adam Whit, Al Samuels, Alex Tindal, Tara DeFrancisco, Jason Chin, Shannon O'Neill, TJ Jagodowski, Dave Pasquesi, Kevin McDonald, Anthony Atamanuik, Michael Orton-Toliver, Jill Bernard, Mel Cowan, Craig Cackowski, Julie Brister, Rich Talarico, Michael J. Gellman, Jorin Garguilo, Mick Napier, Adal Rifai, Farrell Walsh, Kristen Schier, Brian Jim O'Connell, Kevin Scott, Tom Salinksy, Michael Descoteaux, Ryan Millar, Nick Armstrong and Shenoah Allen.

Thanks to all of The Maydays (past and present), to Steve Roe and the whole of Hoopla, to Rachel Blackman (my duo partner for over a decade), to Project2 and the many other groups I have had the pleasure of playing with. Thanks to Liz Peters, Jenny Rowe, Shem Pennant, Megan Ford and Sarah Coleman who took the time to read and feed back on sections and drafts of this book. Thanks to Victoria Hogg for copy-editing, proofreading and constructive insight, and to Fred Deakin who generously designed the cover and typeset the book over many painstaking hours. Thanks also to my husband and favourite person, Tony Harris.

This book is dedicated
to both Jason Chin and Chris Johnston;
each one an inspirational teacher,
mentor and friend.

Foreword

by Susan Messing

So, the lovely Katy Schutte invited me to share a few words about her, which means she trusts me. This is a woman whom I love love LOVE. She immediately endears herself like a leech who is uninterested in sucking your blood, for she is already full. Where I am a gutter full of soggy Autumn leaves, she is fresh Spring green, still attached to the tree. In a world where one can feel overwhelmed by all it has to offer, good and bad, Katy is full-fledged sunshine with no burn. She is an explorer with no judgement. She finds delight in everything – the beauty, the horror, all of it.

When I have had the luxury to perform with Katy, she gobbles up everything: the onstage world is a rich landscape just ready to be tapped, with twistedly delightful characters. Her joy is contagious. Her audiences rejoice because you never ever have to worry about her. She is a partner in the truest sense. We have always had too much fun together.

At this moment, I am missing my friend, Katy.

Did you know that a paragraph only has to be three sentences?

That last sentence is NOT a paragraph.

I have always admired Katy's absolute hunger to learn and to share what she knows. She has travelled the world, studying and teaching and performing. She ascribes to no one school of thought as the 'right' path, but picks and chooses from the buffet what works for her and helps others, and most important, honours her journey of discovery. You know from the moment that you meet her that she is the real deal: someone who celebrates completely not only the joy of her own path, but everyone else's as well. Her great attitude alone is a damn fine reason to read this book.

OMG I think I am in love with Katy. I have to have a talk with my husband. NOW. Now THIS is a life-changing paragraph.

It is beyond difficult to express the ephemeral excitement of improvisational comedy in a book, but if anyone on this planet can make it interesting and helpful on the page, it's going to be Katy. She is a mine of ethically sourced diamonds, at the ready to polish them up, give them to you as empathetic support, and send you on your merry way. Her opinions matter so much because she is that good at what she does, but without the ego that someone normally demonstrates at that proficiency level. She is here to give you courage – for she could not be a better person to understand the struggles that improvisers often face in the performing trenches every week.

So here you are, you supa-cute lover of the art, thinking: "Just get on with the fucking book and shut the fuck up, Messing. Get out of my way so I can read this stuff and apply it like a salve to my burnt performer soul." I get it. I'm in love with her. Relax your crack. I'm almost done. My husband just asked me if Katy's hot.

I have taught Katy, but really, to be completely honest, this lady has taught me far more than I have taught her. She reminds me that learning is never complete, that unintentional comedy is just as valid as intentional, and that if you constantly reapply joy to the mix, you will be making love to Success. This bitch has the goods.

Read this. Then read it again and buy it for a friend and then read it again because you forgot what you read and then read it again and highlight the juicy bits and then read it again and add Bible verses on the side so that you can appear religious. Then go out there and have too much fun on stage and then you can be more like Katy, because Katy is a rockstar and we're getting married.

Susan Messing
Comedy Doula
Susan is an American improvisational theatre performer, teacher and author associated with the Annoyance Theatre and iO Chicago.

Introduction

This is a twelve-week course in improvisation and improvisational thinking. Improvisation is the art (yes, I said art) of making things up as you go along. We will be looking at dramatic and comedic improvisation for the stage.

This book is intended for relative newcomers and experienced longform improvisers to use as a manual for group and/or individual practice.

What is Longform Improvisation?

To people who are brand new to improv:
Longform is a piece of theatre that is made up as we go along. It can be a comedy show but it doesn't have to be.

To people who have come from shortform improvisation:
Shortform improvisation normally either has a director or one of the cast step out to direct a single game. That director tells the cast and the audience the rules of the game.

It might be something like "Every time I say 'new choice', you will alter the sentence you've just said by changing the last word."

> "I'm going to Aldi."
> "New choice."
> "I'm going to the forest."
> "New choice."
> "I'm going to hug you."

This final declaration will become the new reality and the scene will continue. However, in longform, the director is no longer a showman to the audience and a cattle driver for the performers; she is everyone in the show and she is doing the directing internally. If there is a game, it will be discovered as the actors play or it will be suggested in one line of character dialogue at the beginning of the scene (like a secret language).

An example of a longform game might be: I might mention a Twinkie and my scene partner gets excited about the film *Ghostbusters*. Then I try and mention lots of famous foods or props from films and my scene partner can reminisce about those films, getting more and more excited about them. That will be our game that we find or create. In finding it I notice that my scene partner gets excited about *Ghostbusters* when I mention a Twinkie, so I try and prompt her with other films. If I am suggesting the game, I might telegraph the idea like:

"Wow, that Twinkie made you pretty excited about *Ghostbusters*, huh?"

Often longform has a given structure of beats or scenes. The Harold is the famous Chicago form originated by Del Close and it teaches us about bringing characters back, creating links and relationships and exploring theme. There are many more such as Pretty Flower, Slacker, Armando, Deconstruction, La Ronde and so forth, and new ones are being created all the time. You can also perform freeform or montage longform where there is no set structure, or you discover a structure as you go along. Narrative longform tells a linear story and genre longform emulates or parodies a particular author, film director or other artist.

Hello, I'm Katy.

At the time of writing, I've been doing longform improvisation for thirteen years and playing shortform and drama games since I was thirteen years old. That's not very long on a 'veteran improviser' timescale but Malcolm Gladwell would call me an expert as I have more than 10,000 hours under my belt. I have been writing an improv blog since 2011, some of which has been adapted for this book.

Do you remember the day you found out about Santa? (If you don't know what I mean, skip ahead.) For me, it's the same as the day I found out that improv isn't maths. I had a teacher at iO Chicago who totally contradicted what another teacher at iO Chicago said. I really didn't know what to do with that for a while. I had imagined there must be some grand unified theory to improv but it's a case of finding out what works for you without letting fear keep you in too safe a place.

There are different styles of shows, different schools and different philosophies that contradict one another. As a student at any level, there's only so much stuff you can work on at one time. If you were told all the wisdom that experienced improvisers have, right at the beginning, you'd go back to Zumba. Good teachers can sit there with twenty notes in their head and only give you two, because you can work on that many. Some of the guidelines we give new improvisers are just training wheels. You can't ride the bike just yet, but it's great for you to experience what it feels like without your Dad holding the back of it the whole time. Occasionally, then, I will be your Dad in this book, or Santa (welcome back), or your training wheels. At other times I will tell it like it is. Occasionally, I'll be wrong. Happily, 'wrong' is where a lot of the good stuff comes from in improvisation.

I have never tried Zumba.

I have written this book to answer some of the questions that have come up for me or my students. When I teach, people often ask what to do next on their improv journey, how they can find a team, how they can get better on their own or with their team. I've also reached into my darker moments to offer advice for those times when a show goes badly, when we stop enjoying the art form or when we just find it hard.

I hope that you find some useful insights that work for you in this book. Many of the exercises come from other improvisers, some are from me finessing something I've learned, or making an exercise up. I have included a list of my teachers in the hope that I will catch all of them in here somehow.

I'm an improviser who performs on stage. It might be different for you.

- You might want to use improv as a tool in your business.
- You might like improvising because you're a schoolteacher and it's useful to build up a bank of fun exercises that your students can play.
- You might have moved to a new town and want a hobby that helps you find new friends fast.
- You might enjoy the rehearsal part but not the onstage stuff.
- You might be writing or devising a scripted show.

We're not all performers. Improv is a tool for artists and businesses alike. Use it in a way that works for you.

My Origin Story

I'm interested in the origin stories of other improvisers, so here's mine.

School

I discovered improvisation at secondary school. I didn't realise this until years later. We had a teacher called Mrs Smith who wore fluffy slippers and got us to play lots of shortform games (she didn't call them that). I remember her as being sixty, so she was probably twenty-five. I had completely forgotten about this nugget of improv training until I found a school report where I use the word improvisation twice in a twenty-seven word comment.

> "Drama is one of my favourite subjects although I don't feel that we do enough improvisation. My favourite areas are acting from scripts, in groups and improvisation."

I was a well-behaved kid for the most part, although I did get bored easily and – perhaps predictably for a comedian – got bullied a lot. It so happened that the few friends I had were in the other group for Drama lessons, so I skipped my English class and went to their Drama group to get another dose of improvisation. My English teacher was phoning it in by showing VHS in the old top-loading video player and mentally (if not physically) leaving the room.

I learned more by breaking the rules.

I remember a moment where I was playing an air hostess and I just said "tea or coffee" and for whatever reason – context, repetition, character – I got a big laugh. It was a different laugh than the scolding, bullying laugh that I was used to. I felt in control of it and I felt in control of the room. Also, I was having fun with my mates in a place I wasn't really allowed to be.

College

I took Drama again at sixth-form college where I learned the principles of Brecht and Stanislavski with an excellent teacher called Barbara Braithwaite. She used improvisation to get the practitioners' philosophies across to us. I learned for the first time about how to play truthfully and through a thin veil of character (though I wouldn't know or use such terminology for a long time).

I had intended to study visual art but over time I found more and more that I was drawn to the immediate gratification of writing and rehearsing theatre. It was more fun than the lonely five hours of Art homework I would do while I listened to the charts on Radio One.

University

I ditched Art and went to do a Drama BA (Hons) at Hull University. Hull was a dream. I'm sure it still is. At the time it was the best academic university for Drama in the country. The thing is, I really just did the bare minimum in terms of the actual book study and was besotted with all the opportunities we had to be creative. The first year didn't count towards any of our marks and a lot of it was practical acting classes. I spent a week or two with Toby Jones learning clowning and physical theatre, I learned body and text with Nike Imoru and picked up a thousand acting tools. Despite all this, I had never intended to be a performer. Up to this point I thought of myself as a writer (my dad is a writer) and a theatre director. I thought I was bad at acting, so it was better to be on the outside of it. More and more I wrote plays, short sketches and weird postmodern pieces that I could be in as well as make. I started being an auteur.

In the summer of 1999; my first year at university, I went to the Edinburgh Festival Fringe. It was incredible; it literally changed my life. I saw my first longform improv show, *Baby Wants Candy*, the improvised full-band musical from Chicago. I didn't know how it was done, but I went back pretty much every day. I was in Edinburgh the next two summers and I went and saw *BWC* over and over. Though I went to the theatre and to comedy clubs a lot, there was nothing like it where I lived in Hampshire and nothing like it in Hull.

Brighton

It wasn't until my mid-twenties when I was living in the South Coast seaside city of Brighton that I found John Cremer. There was a photocopied flyer on the noticeboard of a small Brighton pub theatre called the Marlborough, with a man on it suggesting that I should go to his improv class. It was the first one I'd come across and I did a workshop day with him. I loved it and joined his Thursday-night drop-in class. Whenever I arrived, there was a small group of other improvisers just finishing their rehearsal.

I wanted to come to that earlier rehearsal. I got to be in a lot of scenes with those people and they were really good. I delivered what I thought was a killer line to a guy called Mark. He responded with an even better one and it felt fantastic. I wasn't beating him, instead we were making something better together. Rachel Blackman, one of the core group, came up to me and suggested I ask John if I could join The Maydays. Apparently, that was the group that was rehearsing earlier. I asked, he said "See you at 6pm next week," and I was in The Maydays. It was a number of months before I got the chance to play on stage. I was annoyed because I thought I was much better than some of the players in the show (ah, the arrogance of youth). Happily, one night, one of the crew bailed and I got a last-minute call at the witchy New Age shop I was working in. I rushed to the badly lit upstairs of The Open House pub. John brought his own lightbulbs to brighten it up. It was a great show. I actually have video. Obviously it's not as good as it was in my mind. We were competently doing shortform and that's it, but it was cool.

Second City, iO, The Annoyance and UCB

After a few months, I became really close friends with Rachel and we decided that we wanted to do some more training. Rachel likes to do things properly, so she found out that the best place to learn improvised comedy was Second City in Chicago. I borrowed a lot of money and we went to do the Second City writing, improv and musical-improv intensives. I loved it. I learned a lot. While we were there, another student asked us if we'd been to the improv school iO. We hadn't. We had not even heard of it, so we went up the road to watch some other improv. I saw TJ and Dave and it was the best thing. It blew my mind. Even though it was played with object work and a blank set, I remembered (still remember) the whole show as a movie. It was one of the most elegant plays I had ever seen and not a word had been written beforehand. This was my – our – new passion. Rachel and I went back to Brighton and in our naivety we booked an hour-long twoprov show. It went very well, so we did it for another eleven years…

I kept playing with The Maydays while I qualified then practised as a massage therapist, worked in the Gardner Arts Centre box office and did the occasional acting job. Three years after Second City, I borrowed more money and went to iO Chicago in 2008. I did the five-week intensive and it turned my whole brain upside down. Rachel and I had been cobbling together our own systems from what we had seen at iO and learned at Second City. This time, most of The Maydays came along. A couple went to The Annoyance which is yet another Chicago improv school with its own brilliant philosophy. We learned together and we got deeper into longform. The year before we went, we were already doing *Mayday! The Musical* with only our own longform training. We won Best Comedy Show at the Brighton Festival, had a local radio sitcom and wrote a lighthearted column for the local paper. The cast of The Maydays changed gradually over the years. We all trained in different places and the company brought over improvisers from the States at least annually to keep developing our work (including the excellent Jason Chin and super-smart Bill Arnett). I was stretching out and working with other people on many different improv projects.

UCB has also been a big influence on my work as I have worked with so many directors and teachers from and within that school. I have performed with The Maydays at the Del Close Marathon in New York and been lucky enough to play with some of UCB's veteran improvisers.

Now

The last twelve+ years with The Maydays is quite a mishmash of memories and people, but it's my improv home. Over this period I've been back to Chicago multiple times and played in *Whirled News Tonight*, *The Armando Diaz Experience*, *Messing With a Friend* and *Baby Wants Candy* among others. I now travel the world performing as well as teaching improv for festivals, in public classes and for businesses, keeping my base in London and working with The Maydays (performing, teaching and directing longform), Project2 (science-fiction longform), Hoopla (teaching and corporate improv), the *Destination* podcast (longform improv) and various other shows. I'm an actor and I pay the mortgage with commercials, theatre and comedy shows, corporate improv training, coaching teams and performing improv. It's a pretty great place to be.

How to Use This Book

Read this book from front to back, doing the weekly exercises as you go along. I have collated essays and exercises in this way so that there is a journey for you to follow. Revisit the various articles and games when you need them. There are solo and group exercises every week so that you can use either or both. Put it in your diary and don't book over it. If you have to, move it rather than cancelling. Choose a space and time where you'll be free from distractions. See it as a course and hold yourself to account to find the time to do it every week. If you do mess up and miss a whole week because something unprecedented happens, don't give up, pick it up and keep going.

Weekly Practice

Read

This book is built like a twelve-week course, so go ahead and read the essays in each chapter every week.

Improvise

There will be questions to fill in and exercises to try. Some will be fun and easy, others might be harder. Some will suit you, some won't. This art form contradicts itself, so try everything and see what works for you.

I have included solo and group exercises with every chapter, so that even if you are isolated where you live you can still rehearse. If you do have a group you can work with, it's sometimes hard to get everyone together on the same day or time. Over the years, I have always found it easier to get people together on the same day every week. Mondays have always been sacred to The Maydays (even though we have switched from evenings to daytimes) and Project2 often do a season of regular rehearsals a few times a year. This book takes you through twelve weeks, so plan every one with your group and/or make space in your diary for solo work.

Brian Jim O'Connell (iO West) recommends doing five minutes of solo improvisation a day because it's much more likely that you'll stick to a tiny length of time than starting out trying to do thirty minutes and quitting early because you failed. Playing a rhyming game while you shower or monologuing before you fall asleep are pretty easy (unless you share a bed). I will suggest specific exercises in every chapter; do them all if you can.

If you are able to do a show in front of an audience too, great!

Watch

How will you know what improv is unless you've seen it? Seeing one show isn't enough. That would be like reading just one book and thinking that qualifies you to write one.

When it's a good show, you get to see collaboration as magic. Watching is also a great way of being part of your local improv community and it will give you opportunities to play with different people, talk about the art and make new chums with similar interests. If you are a performance improviser it's a great way to find out what you like and don't like in terms of style and to find role models and inspiration for your work.

Watching improv is nearly as good as practising, as long as you don't treat it as a passive experience. Whether the show is successful or not, you can be doing improv in your head. You can spot themes, remember character names, decide what you would do next in that situation and log exciting ways of playing and editing.

I understand it can be difficult for some people to watch improv. If you can't afford it, offer to help out in exchange for a ticket or find free shows. If you don't have time, make time. If you're meeting a friend or partner, see a show with them. If you work in the evenings, or there is no live improv near you, watch it online. If you are seriously busy all the time, get up ten minutes earlier and watch a bit. You might live somewhere that doesn't have an improv scene yet. It could be a little early on for me to say "create one" and if it is, there is plenty of stuff online that you can watch. Many theatres have started streaming their shows live, either for free or super-cheap.

If you are busy gigging, then make sure you stay till the end of the show and watch the other acts. If you do have the time, money and inclination, I would really recommend making a pilgrimage to Chicago, New York, London or another huge improv hub or going to a European improv festival to watch improv every night and take classes.

Reflect

Take at least ten minutes to reflect on how you're doing at the end of each week and write down your findings.

> Did you find anything hard or super-easy?
> Was anything ridiculous and didn't make any sense?
> Do you hate/love your work?
> Do you hate/love your team?
> How was rehearsal?
> How was the show you saw?
> What else came up?
> Are there any areas you want to work on?
> Anything else?

Read Improvise Watch Reflect

When you're ready to start your twelve weeks:

- Get a notebook and pen that you like the look of, or carry this book around and write all over it.
- Book time in your diary to rehearse (solo and/or with a group).
- Book an improv show to watch.
- Book ten to twenty minutes in your diary in which to reflect on your first week.
- Start! Read and follow Week One.

"We only get so many scenes in our lifetime, so why go in afraid?"
TJ and Dave

Curse of the Pioneer

This section is specifically for those readers who are teachers or leaders in their improv community. First of all, thank you for reading this when you already know a lot about improv and thank you for still having an open mind.

Perhaps you're the first person in your small community to learn about improv, or perhaps just longform. Either you moved from a big improv scene to a smaller place, or you journeyed to an improv Mecca and want to bring the longform back home. Trent Pancy from Tampere, Finland, lived and studied in Chicago, Neil Curran has been learning in New York for years but lives in Dublin, Ireland, and there are many more pioneers out there.

When I learned longform in Chicago in 2005, I came back to Brighton with Rachel Blackman very excited to teach it to everyone. The problem was that no one there had heard of it or seen it. I attempted to take more classes in London, but there were very few available. There were classes *approaching* longform, but it was narrative, heavily directed, or there was a kind of serious actor corner where the work was closer to Forum theatre. I couldn't find Harolds or sweep edits or tag-outs anywhere I went in London or Brighton. That meant that Rachel and I were attempting to teach what we had learned in the States to The Maydays when they simply hadn't seen longform. We didn't have the vocabulary that we do today and we were often making up our own terminology just to help get the group on board.

Here are my thoughts for the pioneers and for the people who work with them.

Pass on everything you have learned but make sure that you are not giving people a doctrine

Help them to understand that they are individuals who can make a glorious Voltron (giant super-robot) together. You can hold the authority in the room while still keeping an honest balance between the things you're certain of and the things you are still exploring.

There's plenty to watch

When I started, resources online were much more limited. Now, even if you're the first person in your town to improvise, you can still watch hours of excellent longform shows. Chicago twoprov TJ and Dave have a Vimeo channel, Dasariski film loads of their shows and so on. I remember being ridiculously excited when the book *Art by Committee* had a DVD in the back featuring Chicago's tag-edited comedy show Beer Shark Mice and other teams.

Give up control

This is the hardest one. Because Rachel and I led our community through longform in the early years, I still have a little bit of the caretaker left in my work. On a bad day, that means that I can't trust my fellow players; I fill the space a little too quickly. When fun stuff is happening I become the grown-up who's making sense of it all. The thing is, that isn't anyone's fault but mine. If I caretake less but break out and add to the silly and funny too, others will take care of me. If I relent to that tiny gap where others haven't come on stage, they will learn to fill that space because they're not relying on me to do it. In some companies, the leader or director who brought that show together will continue to stay in that position. They will verbally direct the show from inside or outside of scenes and that way, the improv doesn't get to do what it does best, which is become the sum of the people inside of it. If it's always your hard initiation driving the scene, or your voiceover telling the story, you'll get bored of yourself and your cast will settle into that dynamic. Fuck it all up in the best way you can. Get out of the way of your community and join back in as a reactive, supportive player. Try responding more than you initiate, avoid walk-ons unless they really support the show, and allow yourself to take risks where you trust your new group to support you. Make moves you don't yet understand.

Learn from your students

What do they do *better* than you? Even if they're not stronger improvisers yet, I'll bet some of them have better physicality, emotional honesty, rhyming, game (and more) than you.

Your style isn't the only one

Emotional and character players that grow in a 'gamey' community can dislike their own work because they have learned that fast and funny is the aim, and humanity is less valuable. Of course, the perfect show would have all of the above. One of my students from last weekend said: "I'm scared that if I'm honest and speak my own mind on stage, I'll just cry." With the right support, what an incredible scene that would be. Another said: "I can't keep up. When it gets really wacky, I just can't see what is true about it." So she doesn't go on stage at that point. The point when we need her the most; where her truth and emotional honestly would ground a crazy scene and make the funny funnier.

"With great responsibility, comes even more responsibility."
Beautifully misquoted from Stan Lee by one of my students

Week One:
The Basics

There are a lot of rules or guidelines around improvisation but improv is not maths. A rule that proves useful in making great scenes may only work ninety per cent of the time or stop a new improviser from making a choice that could have been hilarious or heartfelt. The basics here are training wheels to help simulate the feeling of being in a successful, funny scene. You can also use them as a checklist to save a scene that is not going well.

The most useful basic is fun. Improv is fun. If you're having fun, your co-stars are having fun and the audience is enjoying watching you: you are doing great.

The Basics

Listen

Listening is the most important aspect of communication. If you don't listen, then how can you respond in a valuable way? Listening doesn't just mean hearing the words, it also means noticing body language and emotional undertones. Try listening until the end of the sentence and not formulating your response until you have heard everything the other person wants to say.

Get on the same page

We can quickly get on the same page as other people. The reason improvisation is such an interesting art form is that we are creating something together right now. It is different to what any of the individuals would have created on their own. If you have a great idea, leave space for the other improviser to join you and expand your idea. If you don't have an idea, add to what you have learned from listening to your scene partner and build the scene together.

'Yes-and'

Sometimes, we can be a little quick to judge an idea before it has been fully explored. However 'bad' ideas are often at the root of or the inspiration for good ones.

We can avoid conflict by saying yes and have more comedy and fun than argument in the scene. A great example is the sword-fighting scene between Inigo Montoya and The Dread Pirate Roberts in *The Princess Bride*. They are verbally admiring each other's sword-fighting skills while trying to kill one another.

Initially teachers tell you that everything must be met with a literal 'yes-and' because we want you to accept and build on what your scene partner is giving you. We give you exercises where we make 'yes-and' a bit of text that you have to use at the beginning of every line.

PLAYER ONE: "You need to stop eating cake, Annette."

PLAYER TWO: "Yes – and I will give up fizzy drinks too."

Later on, you will be able to see the subtleties of what is actually blocking the scene and what makes for a better one. You can say 'no' as the character, but 'yes' as the actor.

PLAYER ONE: "You need to stop eating cake, Annette."

PLAYER TWO: "I'll just have a couple more pieces."

They are saying 'no' to stopping eating, but 'yes' to the suggestion that they are a character who likes to eat a lot of cake.

Denial isn't something only beginners do. At the start, it will be as obvious as:

PLAYER ONE: "I am a police officer."

PLAYER TWO: "No, you're a plumber."

Much later it can be something as subtle as:

PLAYER ONE: "Let's arrest this man."

PLAYER TWO: "Troy – he's too fast for us."

It sounds like an offer, but it's also an excuse to not arrest this man. Try arresting him while he runs away and that's fine, but don't find reasons not to do something your partner suggests. I did this in a show two nights ago. I found a reason not to jump on a sex swing with my husband. He offered that he hadn't screwed it in very well to the ceiling, so I thought it wasn't a good idea. A realistic response, but comedy would rather we put ourselves in trouble.

Agree with the reality

If you're in a scene set in a McDonald's and you've never been to one, it doesn't matter; this is your McDonald's. This one can work any way you like: more staff than customers, only salads, oak booths, comfortable sofas and table service. That is how this

McDonald's works. The important thing about this is that everyone agrees with the new world rules. If we have table service in McDonald's now, that's how it works for the whole show.

Commit

How you say what you say is often the thing that inspires people to get on board. Imagine someone getting on their knees with a wedding ring and half-heartedly asking you to marry them. I mean: you wouldn't. But if it seemed like a defining moment in their life, you'd at least have to think about it. Committing to an idea doesn't mean you have to love it yourself but it shows that idea in its best light so that others can enjoy it. There must be something about it that made it pop into your head in the first place?

When beginners fail to commit, they put a question mark at the end of their offer, do a face that suggests what they said was a mistake or just look horribly awkward and apologetic in their physicality. More experienced improvisers might undercommit by calling out something that went 'wrong' with the scene: "Well, that went weird." It might even be hard to tell whether it's the character or the performer who's making the offer, but it will get a laugh and therefore release some of the tension in a scene – tension that might have made the scene more successful in the long term.

Know

A good way of committing in improvisation is to play an expert. In improvisation we are always making things up as we go along, but sometimes we don't have the facts at our disposal. Perhaps someone says: "Ah, Doctor, thank goodness you're here." What on earth are you going to do now? This is scary because you don't know the first thing about medicine, but you know that you need to say yes to the offer. You might want to say: "Yes, I am a doctor and it's my first day."

Perhaps that feels safer, but if it's your first day as a doctor, you should still know all about your chosen profession. It can feel like a safety net, in case it all goes wrong but here's the fun news: you *can't* get it wrong. You can be any kind of doctor you like because you are in your own universe and even if you don't know the word for colonoscopy in real life, in improv it can be called 'a poop-piping procedure' and everyone will be on board. So, instead of it being your first day, be an expert, be the best doctor you could possibly be. "Yes, I am a doctor, I am the foremost doctor of Spilifics and my speciality is Doodlebing."

Make it look intentional

Commitment is the basic level of selling your idea or performance. Later on, when we have got over apologising or doing a cringe face when we're not sure about our offers, we can make every move look intentional. If your body goes to do something (like editing) and you don't follow, it looks like a mistake. If you talk over someone, it looks like a mistake. If you keep talking over them, or keep walking when you meant to edit, it looks like a choice. Lean into anything that wasn't supposed to go that way, signalling to the audience that everything is an active choice, as if your theatre director planned the show or rehearsal this way for a reason.

I would also add the following basics that we'll look at in detail later with exercises:

Make your scene partner look good (and give them a good time)

If you're making your scene partner look good and they're doing the same for you, the whole show will look good. The better you know another improviser, the more you can give them the improv they like to play on stage and everyone will have more fun.

Trust that they're doing the same for you (even if they're not)

If you believe that everyone is making you look good, you will enjoy the show a lot more and be more giving and less competitive. There must be a reason that they gave you this offer? What opportunity do they want to give you?

Look after yourself

Even if you don't have a strong idea to bring to the stage, choosing an attitude or character trait can give your partner something to work from. Being neutral is a difficult place to start a scene.

Serve the show (not at the expense of your cohorts)

The show is your ultimate master. If you have a few choices in your head, go for the one that will make the show more successful. If someone has made a move that you don't understand, mirror that move, or clarify what it might be so that nothing is left abandoned or unsupported.

Give Them What They Want (but Not What They Expect)

This is true of both audiences and your scene partner. We'll talk about audiences later. Bizarrely perhaps, giving someone what they want on stage is not as common as you'd think. Here are some ways that you can give you scene partner exactly what they want.

Game

We've talked about 'yes, and' and how it's sometimes a stronger comedy choice to say no and end up doing it anyway. Look beneath the surface of the text and see what the other improviser wants from you.

"Jill, don't keep going on about the sales reports" actually means "Jill, keep going on and ON about the sales reports."

That's what the other improviser wants from you. They want you to find any trigger to get back into talking about the sales reports. That's an example of Game of the Scene and how by playing (and heightening) the game, you're giving your scene partner what they want.

Emotion

If your scene partner has made a choice to be scared about something, what do they want from you? I see a lot of scenes where the responder will try and do the human thing of calming them down, but that's not really where comedy or drama lie. Mirroring your partner's emotion is a really strong way of supporting it. We are both terrified. Or you could choose to make it worse. Making something worse is a great way of birthing comedy. If they're scared of the dark, sympathise as the character, but keep finding reasons to put them in the dark, or remind them how scary the dark is. "Wow, I used to be scared of the dark too, but now I feel like I'm physically strong enough to take on any monsters. You should think about getting strong too, I'm not sure you could bust one right now."

Sanity

The default (and not great) way of dealing with crazy onstage characters or choices is to call them out as crazy: "You're crazy!" That doesn't give the improviser much to work with. You might have helped them define their choice as 'insane' but there are no real specifics in there. I was taking a weekend class with Susan Messing in a small, hot ex-office space in London's Brick Lane when she offered a few excellent ways of playing with crazy. My favourite one was to treat them like a genius. If there's a girl who only screams "Spiders" at the top of her voice and occasionally licks people on the face, why not have this person in the think-tank of some huge corporate enterprise? Every lick and scream is super-useful to the business and keeps sparking ideas in the employees.

> "Cliff, we just don't know what motivates our clientele any more!"
> "Spiders!"
> "You're right, young lady, we need to set up some kind of web of support! Boy, is she smart. I don't know how we coped without you, Margarite."

You are supporting your partner in this way and telling them that their choice is amazing. In a Project2 show, we had a very weird character who would only draw penguins and found it difficult to talk. Of course, they were the most high-status character in the show and by inspiring other characters, they saved the Earth.

Objects

Object work (or space work) is the improv word for miming; where we pretend we are touching and using objects in the space. There can often be small denials in the way people respond to object initiations. Try performing a bunch of scenes where one of you starts a mimed interaction with the environment, or think back on the most recent object scenes you saw or played in.

Nine times out of ten, the person who is joining the scene will criticise and shut down the action.

To an actor miming breakfast-making:
>	"Why are you making breakfast this early?!"

To an actor miming fitting a door:
>	"You're fitting that door wrong."

To an actor vacuuming:
>	"*Stop* vacuuming."

At first it seems like a strong idea; you're telling us what the action is so that we're all on the same page and you're making a strong emotional choice; to disagree or be overbearing. But think about that other improviser. They have created a whole world out of nothing, whether it's frying an egg, fitting a door or moving a vacuum cleaner around. Now you have come in and basically (or literally) told them to stop doing that thing. If you haven't actually *stopped* them, you have made the scene one where you will just be talking about that object and *how* you should both be interacting with it. "If you just put the hinges a little lower…" I'm not saying these scenes never work, but why not try something that is more positive, supportive and builds on what they started with? Try doing something physically complementary to what they're doing. If they appear to be making breakfast, go cut some bread and put it in the toaster, or get that coffee on. If they're fitting a door, go measure the height of the frame, or take the drill off charge. Sometimes you won't have a clue what they're doing; they just appear to be moving their hands around. Well, they may not have made a strong choice about it yet, and even if they have; if you don't have a clue, it's unlikely the audience will either. What does their mime look most like and how can your movements define it for the improvisers and the audience?

What do they want? They want your help in defining their movement and your assistance in laying down the building blocks of a scene.

I don't know what they want!

It can feel limiting if you're not really sure what your partner wants. I have students who were worried about going on stage in case they 'messed up' and misunderstood what was wanted from them. It's more important that you do *something* than worry about what is right. If you feel like the other actor wants something specific from you in a scene, you can always 'yes' without 'and'-ing for a couple of lines so that they can get their idea out there. But if it's not really clear in the first few lines, just go ahead and flesh out the reality together. Try to offer something that you would want if the roles were reversed. What response or decision would you like from that other person to ensure you had a fun scene? Stopping you from doing what you're doing, denying that it is true or calling you crazy is unlikely to be a fun choice.

Super-agreement

I love this term. The first thing most of us learn is to say 'yes-and' but this is like the boss level of 'yes-and'. Imagine that instead of just agreeing with the reality, this is literally the best suggestion you ever heard and you cannot wait to climb on board and build it even higher!

This is an example of lack of agreement from a Project2 workshop in Finland:

> *Two young men on a street corner.*
> PLAYER ONE: "You can't be the boss of me any more."
> PLAYER TWO: "Oh YEAH? (*Pulls a gun out.*)"

Literally the only information we have is that the second character won't be the boss again. The second line is undoing that. Just to restate, the actor might well be making a game move that says "Come and be the boss of me" and that's fine, but unless it's obviously the case, go for super-agreement:

> PLAYER ONE: "You can't be the boss of me any more."
> PLAYER TWO: "I know, man, since your growth spurt, there's no way I can
> challenge you."

Super-agreement can be used to demonstrate examples of how you are weak in comparison, or tell us why you are no longer the boss of this guy. Add – don't reframe or take away.

Another example of super-agreement:

Player One: "Tom, you're a total asshole."
Player Two: "I am the biggest asshole – did you see how I spilled my red wine on the carpet and didn't clean it up?"

Be a Nice Person

Improvisers are almost always nice people. Our lives are spent finding ways to talk and move in such a way that makes the people around us have a nice time. The philosophy of treating one another like 'artists, geniuses and poets,' as Del Close puts it, has become a way of being in the real world. If I ever go to another country to do improv, I am immediately plugged into the community there. I will have somewhere to stay, people to eat and drink with, shows to play in and students to teach. We are generous to one another and we immediately trust one another. If a friend asks me if someone I have never met can stay at my house I will probably say no. If they are an improviser, I would have no worries saying yes. Murderers: take note. Just say you're an improviser.

With improvisation, there's no use in playing a cunning power game, psyching out the competition for roles or slagging off other shows (even if you don't think they're very good).

It definitely took some brain-changing for me to be a more giving, trusting person, but the upside is that these days I rarely get jealous or competitive. If someone I know is doing well; that's really great for me. It means I have more opportunities to do well because I know someone in a good position.

> "The grass is always greener where you water it."
> Anon

You will help yourself if you are nicer. I have noticed that improvisers who have spent a few years doing improv can be annoyed about how other people are doing. They have a sense of entitlement, that they should be on a higher rung by now. But of course, there is no real ladder, just who you know, who has seen you play and who you get on well with. Keep playing, be kind about other shows, try and find the positive in things you don't like and watch and advertise other people's projects when you can. This is how we build community. I used to whinge about Keith Johnstone because I learned improv in a different way, but now I just accept that there are different ways into our art form. I do my best to learn a little bit from every corner so that I can play in as many shows and styles as possible. If for some reason you really dislike a school, a show or a performer, it may be time to ask yourself why. It will nearly always be more to do with you than them.

Have you heard of the Dutch Reach? Cyclists can get seriously injured by car doors being opened in front of them by drivers and passengers who don't check the outside of the car first. Dutch drivers have been taught for decades that they should use the hand furthest from the car door to open it. It means that their bodies are automatically turned around and in a better position to spot cyclists that may be passing. I like to think that the practice of being a nice person is like the Dutch Reach: build it in to how you function and you won't even have to think about it any more. That way, fewer people get hurt.

Using your dislike for good

I have a general dislike of 'clowning'. I also find it annoying when people say "I've created this new character." Let's undo those negatives.

I like trust on stage, so if I'm watching a clown show, I feel uneasy about the unpredictability of being screwed with by someone I don't know. I don't like looking like an idiot. I never got by on being pretty, I always got by on my smarts, so if I'm made to look stupid, I don't have anything left. I cease to be compelling or attractive (in my eyes). So rather than just hating clowning and psychoanalysing myself, I ask what is successful about that particular clowning show.

- He has amazing physicality.
- Everyone else in this room is having a great time.
- He is really brave.
- He has so much presence.

I can put all of those things into action in my work. I can work on my physicality, presence and bravery.

Then I ask myself what I'm scared of.

- Looking like I'm stupid (I'm fine with *looking* stupid, but not with looking like *I'm* stupid).
- Having an audience dislike me.
- Not being compelling enough.

How do I put these elements into action in my work? I make choices where I play stupid characters, I put myself in embarrassing situations in scenes, I deliberately make point-of-view choices that will likely offend the audience. What is the outcome? I scare myself, I push my boundaries and I am giving my scene partners something fun to play off.

Let's do this process for "I've created a new character".

Good things:

- She has found a catchphrase that's making people laugh.
- She has dressed in such a way that this character comes alive.
- She is doing a great job of keeping the character consistent.
- She is owning the room.

What am I scared of?

- Being inconsistent with character.
- Not having enough depth in my characters to make them believable.
- Enjoying my characters enough to use them in a scripted show.

How do I put the things I do like and the things I'm scared of into action? I create vocal and physical tags that lead me back into a character and help them be consistent in an improv show. I write down good phrases that I used as an improvised character and make a scripted solo show using these. I practise exercises to make sure stereotyped characters can be given depth.

Now it's your turn:

What school of improv, improv show or improviser bugs you?

```
┌ ─ ─ ─ ─ ─ ─ ─ ─ ─ ─ ─ ─ ─ ─ ─ ─ ─ ─ ┐
│                                      │
│                                      │
│                                      │
│                                      │
└ ─ ─ ─ ─ ─ ─ ─ ─ ─ ─ ─ ─ ─ ─ ─ ─ ─ ─ ┘
```

But what is good about it? Suggest at least three things.

```
┌ ─ ─ ─ ─ ─ ─ ─ ─ ─ ─ ─ ─ ─ ─ ─ ─ ─ ─ ┐
│                                      │
│                                      │
│                                      │
├ ─ ─ ─ ─ ─ ─ ─ ─ ─ ─ ─ ─ ─ ─ ─ ─ ─ ─ ┤
│                                      │
│                                      │
├ ─ ─ ─ ─ ─ ─ ─ ─ ─ ─ ─ ─ ─ ─ ─ ─ ─ ─ ┤
│                                      │
│                                      │
│                                      │
└ ─ ─ ─ ─ ─ ─ ─ ─ ─ ─ ─ ─ ─ ─ ─ ─ ─ ─ ┘
```

Why does it bug you? What are *you* scared of?

```
┌ ─ ─ ─ ─ ─ ─ ─ ─ ─ ─ ─ ─ ─ ─ ─ ─ ─ ─ ┐
│                                      │
│                                      │
│                                      │
└ ─ ─ ─ ─ ─ ─ ─ ─ ─ ─ ─ ─ ─ ─ ─ ─ ─ ─ ┘
```

How can you combat these fears through action?

```
┌ ─ ─ ─ ─ ─ ─ ─ ─ ─ ─ ─ ─ ─ ─ ─ ─ ─ ─ ┐
│                                      │
│                                      │
│                                      │
└ ─ ─ ─ ─ ─ ─ ─ ─ ─ ─ ─ ─ ─ ─ ─ ─ ─ ─ ┘
```

The Solo Journey

You may be taking the path through this book on your own without a performance team or practice group of any kind. Perhaps you want to perform longform improvisation as a solo artist. Otherwise I've provided exercises for one person so that you can work on your technique individually in order to improve your group experience. There are many skills within improv that can be honed by running exercises on your own.

Solo improvisation is almost a different art form than improv with other players. In group improvisation, you are working with the other actors to build your world one brick at a time. With solo improv there is no back and forth so you build alone. You might – like me – just want to use solo improvisation as some extra rehearsal between shows. Meeting once a week with a team might not be enough to keep you on the ball or advance your work. You might not have a group at this point, or maybe you live somewhere where there aren't many other improvisers and doing solo work is a great way to get experience while the scene expands around you.

I have never done a solo improv show (though I have done stand-up and theatre solos), but I have directed them, coached them, watched them, taken classes in them and – like most of us – performed scenes on my own in an ensemble show. I worked for a while on solo shows with Jinni Lyons and Constantine Pavlou and taught public classes for others with the odd one-off here and there for new solo performers. One was musical, one a monoscene and another an exploration of different solo presentation styles like interactive monologues (one half of a conversation), character monologues, playing multiple characters and so forth. As Jill Bernard will tell you, solo improvisation can be whatever you want it to be because it's your show.

> "Your weaknesses are your strengths and your strengths are your double-strengths."
> Jill Bernard

For example, you can steamroll yourself as much as you like and your offers don't have to be obvious because you already know what you're going for.

The risks – I can't think of a kinder word – with solo improvisation are sameness and smugness. I normally work with solo improvisers on how to surprise and inspire themselves. Take risks in your character choices and push yourself into scenes without a plan. Give yourself offers and allow yourself time to react to them. You could have a technician and/or a musician who will be your show buddy. If the lights or music are moody and dark, push your scenework into that feel or make a strong choice to play against it. The other player in your solo improvisation show is the audience. Use the physical room and all the people in it to steer you. If there is a woman with a strange laugh in the audience, play a character that might embody her (she doesn't need to know). Make sure your show is affected by the circumstances around it in order to keep it from being stilted, safe or smug.

I have written in Week Two: How to Rehearse Solo about planning your solo practice without an external director. Your critic and director brains need to be out of the room in order to play and explore. You can evaluate afterwards, or at pre-chosen points in your rehearsal. You might find it helps to video yourself. Perhaps not even to watch back, but to step up your game for that outside eye. Performing in a vacuum can be really hard in rehearsals. It might even be a good idea to find another solo artist or a few and spend time being an audience for one another.

Warm-ups
Here are some suggested warm-ups. There are more throughout the book, but something from each category should get you into the right headspace to improvise longer scenes or a run of scenes.

Physical
Have a stretch then dance to a song.
Have a slow-motion fight playing several characters. Keep alternating between the combatants to play each strike and reaction.

Mental/writing the show

PREMISE LAWYER

Think of a ridiculous concept like 'Slugs are Smarter than People' then justify that statement. The rules for this game are that you can't make up things that go against science and you must use real-world logic and reason to explain the premise. Challenge yourself if you find holes in your own logic.

> "Slugs are smarter than people. Their goals in life are merely to eat, grow and reproduce. While we are worried about our egos, about falling in love, having enough money to pay our bills and about our terrible impact on the environment and our hideous overpopulation, slugs are moving at the right pace. Without the ability to 'rush' or achieve complex goals, slugs can merely move from one place to another in order to feed themselves. They do not have the mental capacity to 'worry' about the outcome of searching for food; they merely do it. How much easier would life be if we merely moved towards what we wanted, achieved it and set the next goal? How about if we didn't see the coming of salt, of dry weather and predators? The slug is smarter because it is unaware."

Character

CLINGY PRIEST

Before you begin this exercise (which I learnt at iO), write down ten or more adjectives on separate bits of paper. For example:

> Ambitious
> Whimsical
> Steadfast
> Lonely

Now write down ten or more professions on other pieces of paper that seem fun to play. For example:

> Astronaut
> Marine biologist

Security guard
Reflexologist

Set a timer to go off at thirty-second intervals. Every time your alarm goes, pick out an adjective and profession at random and perform a monologue from that character. For example, you might pick 'Whimsical Astronaut'. If thirty seconds feels like a stretch, make them shorter; it's a warm-up, not a show.

Emotion and subtext/acting

Think back to one of your Clingy Priest monologues. Choose your favourite. Now imagine that you were the other character in that scene. React as the person this monologue was directed at. Do it without talking, although you might make as if to speak but not get a word in. How do you feel about the words that have been said? Perhaps you touch objects in that setting or physically interact with that character.

Setting the scene

Tour Guide

I learnt this from Steve Roe. Pull an imaginary curtain to one side and picture a location (or get a call-out from the internet or a word-generation app). You are the tour guide for this location. Describe your environment in great detail, including the smell, sound and texture of the place. Explain the history of various objects and sights. Take questions from your imaginary entourage if you get stuck, to buy you time, or just for fun.

"Here we are in Her Majesty's Zeppelin. We are currently flying at 2000 feet. As you can see, the beautiful fields of England are mapped out below us in a patchwork of colour. The rapeseed in yellow, the lavender in purple. That is Corley's Farm down there on the right. The one with the large outbuilding and all the cows in the field. Corley was accused of murder but never convicted, he moved out in 1983 to this beautiful stretch of Hampshire that lies at the foot of the South Downs. Ah, your cocktails have arrived. Whose is the Bloody Mary? Please take a coaster. To your right, sir..."

Congratulations! You've made it to the end of Week One. Let's go through our weekly practice checklist.

Read

Did you read the chapter? I bet you did.

Improvise

Here are this week's exercises.

Listen
HEADLINES

Work with a partner. One invents a newspaper headline such as "Traffic Busiest on Record", the other listens to the end of the sentence and invents a second headline starting with the last word used. For example:

PLAYER ONE: "Traffic Busiest on Record."
PLAYER TWO: "Record Shop Set to Close."
PLAYER ONE: "Close Your Mouth When Eating, Say Experts."
PLAYER TWO: "Experts Deny Imminent Meteor Impact with Earth."
PLAYER ONE: "Earth Best Planet in Solar System, Say NASA."

Tip: Don't worry about the validity of your headlines. The exercise is about listening, not accuracy of information. It is also super-fun!

Get on the same page
MIND MELD

Work with a partner or with a group in a circle. Two people step forward (A and B) and each think of a word. They count together "1, 2, 3" then announce their words at the same time.

A: "Bench."
B: "Tree."

Both people take a few seconds to think of a word that will make sense of both these words, or join them together in some way. When both people are ready, count together "1, 2, 3" and announce your new word at the same time.

A: "Wood."
B: "Park."

Continue until you manage to say the same word at the same time!

A: "Woodchips."
B: "Playground."

A: "Slide."
B: "Slide."

Then celebrate! We like to dance about and sing a Mind Meld celebration song when we hit the same word:

"Mind Meld
It was a Mind Meld
It happens all the time
It was a Mind Meld."

Tip: Don't panic if you can't land on the same word or if it takes a long time. I've given a simple example to show you how the game works and it might take a lot longer than four goes to say the same word. Really it's about listening carefully and starting to adapt to someone else's way of thinking. The process itself is both the achievement and the fun of the exercise. Often, other players in the circle will have thought of the same word, but not be one of the two calling out. Great; you're all thinking the same way!

'Yes-and'

WOULDN'T IT BE GREAT IF...

With one or more other people, start a conversation with the words "Wouldn't it be great if…" Finish the sentence with a crazy idea like:

> "Wouldn't it be great if worms ruled the Earth?"
> "Wouldn't it be great if coffee came out of the tap?"
> "Wouldn't it be great if giants existed?"

It's very easy to shoot these ideas down. Worms might be pretty bad at running the Earth as they're not too smart, not everyone likes coffee, and giants might be tough to fit on public transport. But let's try instead to be positive, to say 'yes, and' to these ideas. In that instance the conversation might go:

> A: "Wouldn't it be great if worms ruled the Earth?"
> B: "Yes, and they would spell out words with their bodies to tell us what to do."
> C: "Yes, and they would suck baddies down into the earth by strategically creating sinkholes."
> D: "Yes, and they would be cheap to dress and accommodate as they're only small."

Tip: You can try this with serious conversations too. Is there a product or initiative you are working on? What would it look like if there were only positive outcomes?

Commit

STAND AND DELIVER

In a group, have one person at a time stand up in front of the others and deliver a line that they have been given. The line can be anything. Let's say we give them the line: "It looks like bread is getting popular." After one person has delivered the line in the most captivating way they feel they can, everyone else applauds. The person who delivered the line must stay standing and receive the applause before leaving the stage and sitting back down. Perhaps it sounds easy, but it's amazing how reticent we are to stand and enjoy the praise. You may just go and sit down before it has finished, or you may feel your body jolt as you want to sit down but know that you aren't allowed.

Know

EXPERT INTERVIEW

In your group, have one person play the interviewer on a TV chat show and another player be an expert in a particular subject. Using an animal and a sport is a fun way to create a new expertise. For example, you might have an expert in teaching scrimshaw[1] to sparrows. The interviewer can make up an appropriate name for the show and ask the expert a series of questions about their life and work. The important thing here is that the expert must play just that and know the answers to all of the questions. They will make up their backstory, their techniques and so forth on the spot using a lot of specifics. They might even read from their book or take questions from the audience. You will find that knowing is a lot more fun and productive than not knowing or being worried that you'll appear stupid.

Super-agreement

Play a scene where there would likely be conflict and find reasons to constantly agree and get along with the other character.

Use your own suggestions or try:

- A contract killer and her target.
- A person who has just hit another driver's car.
- Two shoppers who both want the last coat in their size.

When we're a little more experienced in improv, we get pretty good at hiding our denials. In real life, the young kleptomaniac takes an extra £20 from the till and gets caught, whereas a smart financier spends years bleeding money from a multi-billion-pound company. You can justify your denials with game, with the filter of your character and so forth, but you're still putting barriers in the way of joy and super-agreement.

---

1   Scrimshaw is carving images into wood or bone.

Super-agreement is not the only way to play, but get into the habit of using it as a default. Stronger choices can override super-agreement when you think they would be more fun.

Watch

Did you manage to see a show?

What was it?

Reflect

Write down your notes or thoughts on what you read, saw or did this week.

Week Two:
Trust
and Practice

This chapter is about the practicalities of rehearsal; how and why we rehearse, who should lead the sessions, how to warm up and what to work on. I'll talk about building good muscle memory and excellent habits so that when you're on stage your job is even easier and more fun. Rehearsals build trust with your team and allow a safe space for you to play and discover.

Why Rehearse Improv?

Why warm up or rehearse at all? Surely you're making it all up anyway, so what's the point? The reason for doing rehearsals is to get better at making things up on the spot. Just making things up on the spot isn't always easy. Get into good habits and build a muscle memory for good improv practice.

It's much harder to have clear goals in improvisation. In science, there is a proof that your solution is correct. You know when you are done. In sports, there are literally scores that tell you who won. We have competitive improv, but the scoring is in favour of comedy and crowd-pleasing and is part of the entertainment itself, not usually a mark of success or failure at all. Nor are you the best judge of your work. You are on stage with a head full of criticism and ego just trying to do good work and support your fellow improvisers. The other performers are in the same situation. They will have a feeling about how well the show went but it may or may not be true. Also, you're making stuff up, so if you delivered a really good scene, you can't repeat those lines again. You can only repeat the behaviour that resulted in a successful moment.

> "Train hard, fight easy."
> Alexander Suvorov

Build muscle memory

There really is a muscle memory for improvisation. Longform teacher Kevin Scott talks about it in terms of 'traps'. It's not that veteran improvisers are naturally much better at improvisation, but that they've had so much experience that they are more aware of where all the traps are; where they might come across difficulties. The more we exercise good scenes, the more likely good scenes are to happen when we're on stage. Musicians do scales, sportsmen and women exercise different muscles. It's the same for us. Our muscles are basic improv skills like listening, agreement and building a reality together.

Perform

Shows are also like rehearsals because improv is never 'finished' like a play. Performing is the most useful way of learning to improvise and I'd warn against rehearsing forever before you put your work up on stage. The very act of putting your work on stage – and having it observed – changes it. The change happens in a dynamic sense because of course it will be different, it's improvised. The quieter people in rehearsal might suddenly become braver with adrenaline and really step up. The self-assured improviser may get overwhelmed and be less of a driver than normal. Your generous friend may have their dad in the audience and make a lot of corny jokes to try and come across as the 'funny one' – perhaps sacrificing her fellow players or the integrity of the scene in the process. I would advise getting your show on stage as quickly as you can. Find out how you all play when there is an audience, so you know what to work on in your rehearsals.

Write down what you are currently working on

For example, this is what I am focusing on this week:

Letting My Partner Respond

I sometimes get so excited that I don't give my scene partner long enough to have a reaction to my offer. As soon as I see that they understand what I'm going for, I start up again before they can digest or build, sometimes literally interrupting their dialogue. It's out of excitement usually, rather than mistrust, but listening and waiting for their response is going to make it easier for both of us.

Choosing to Be Physical

My favourite thing to do in improvisation is to make ridiculous physical choices. In a recent show I was a computer-game character walking into walls and then thrusting against another computer-game character (and then a wall). In the same show I was one of the new evil owners of Castle Greyskull and got around the building by climbing the walls with suckers on my hands and feet. Physical scenes are so fun, but without making a strong choice to play that way before I go on stage, I will forget and get cerebral.

BEING AWESOME AT NAMES

Both in giving awesome names (my unimaginative go-tos are Geoff and Sarah) and remembering all the names. I told myself a long time ago that I am 'bad' at names but I have since realised that doesn't help me in real life or on stage.

I played a murder-mystery show recently with another improviser who told me that he didn't do Harolds because the 'names thing' was so intimidating. I have done a half-arsed mnemonic for people for the past few years and blamed my inadequacy on face blindness. I can learn everyone's name in Week 1 of a course but then I have to start again in Week 2 because everyone changed their clothes and if there are three bald guys or three women with long blonde hair I'm stuffed. I've decided that although my face blindness might be true, it is also a terrible excuse for forgetting names.

Now I've doubled down on names. I can listen to the scene at the same time as creating a really convoluted way of remembering what this character was called. I use mnemonics, so when I taught my drop-in class yesterday, I remembered David as being my dad (who has that name), Claudia as being a cloud with an ear and Jason running through the streets like he was in the (Jason) *Bourne Identity*. Keeping at it and putting the effort in has already started to pay off. I can now remember the names of my students as well as their character names from the day or week before but it's ongoing work and takes up a lot of my brain. Hopefully one day, names will become improv muscle memory and it will be less of an effort.

Exercise

Identify three things you are working on.

> What do you find difficult?
> What do your fellow performers do that you think is amazing?
> What would you like to be better at?
> What is going to take forever to get good at so what's the point?
> Anything else?

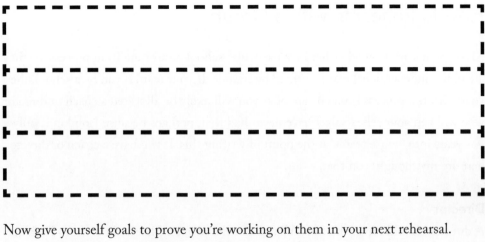

Now give yourself goals to prove you're working on them in your next rehearsal.

    Did I play a gender I'm not today?

    Did I initiate three times or more?

    Did I play low status in more than one scene?

    Did I make a big physical choice in a scene?

    Did I manage to do at least one voice that was different from mine?

If your goals are at odds with what your coach/director wants, put them to one side and pick them up later on. Do them in shows and do them at home. Work those muscles. If you don't know how to improve on something, keep a note of it and hopefully I'll cover it in one of the coming weeks.

You will have huge improv muscles.

How to Rehearse with a Group

Most groups are formed either by a particular school and/or audition process, or they are indie (independent) teams formed by friends. If your team is run by a school, then your rehearsal process is taken care of as you will likely be allocated a coach or director who will run your rehearsals. I have never had that, perhaps because London is only a few years into 'house teams' at the point of writing this. If you have a coach or director, here are my thoughts on that.

Director

A director should direct the SHOW and not the people. I learned this from Rich and Rebecca Sohn. The Maydays are all at a similar level of improv, so it can feel weird if your team are telling you how to improvise or vice versa. The Sohns had learned a lesson that it's not okay to give notes to your fellow players. It just breeds resentment. We all make different choices in improv and they're all good.

I directed *Oh Boy! The Quantum Leap Show* for The Maydays. It was a longform show based on the TV series *Quantum Leap* where Sam Beckett time-travels through history, striving to put right what once went wrong. I was careful to make sure that I wasn't critiquing anyone's improv, but honing the sort of choices that would produce a *Quantum Leap* feel and story. For example, *Quantum Leap* is the most anti-improv show ever. We didn't realise till we started but the protagonist, Sam, has to ask a lot of questions and pretend he has no idea what's going on. In improv, you mostly need to look like you know exactly what's going on and it's a stronger choice to be an expert than for it to be your (yawn) 'first day'. It's hard for Sam to drive the story because he has no idea why he's there and what he has to put right. We also didn't want to be hampered by narrative, so it was about finding tropes that fit the feel of the show instead of telling everyone what was about to happen. Al can be *wrong*, offers can be *dropped* and the show works. Hell, Al is only ever seen by Sam, children and pets. Most of the cast spend the show ignoring one improviser! The driving force of the show is that Sam follows his heart and his moral compass.

Another example was a show I directed called *Silly String Theory*. Though I was directing, I brought in longform teacher Ryan Millar and a few others to coach us during rehearsals. The show was my vision but there were skills we all needed to work on. In that show we discovered that because it was a 'slice of life' form, we didn't want to have anything extraordinary happen. For example, you couldn't have a bunch of Gods chatting unless you justified that that was a novel someone was writing or a play that someone was in. Again, that's the director narrowing choices to fit the form, not just raising everyone's general skill level.

Coach

This is the sticky one. My experience of coaching is that there is a group or cast that brings someone in to raise their game. The group has already decided what they want. Sometimes that is as vague as "Get better at improv" and sometimes it's as specific as "We want to do a rap game in our shortform show." The word 'coach' is the same as it is in sports because it is the same role. There is a team and it's your job to make them win. An improv *teacher* supports failure (makes you comfortable with it, so you can get better) whereas an improv coach supports success (we are going to nail this). You can still say "Do it like this, not like that", but the group ultimately has the choice. You really need a discussion about exactly what the group want out of the coaching. And that's different to the teacher role. Afterwards, the group can decide what parts of that coaching fit the show or the team.

I believe that the coach should have the authority in the room. They are not one of the team, they are the disciplinarian. You do what the coach says, that's what you're paying them for.

Running your own rehearsals

Rachel Blackman and I (Katy and Rach) were directed by co-Mayday Alexis Gallagher for several years: he would run exercises with us, and then do longer and longer sets. We spent at least a year setting every scene in a car because he wanted us to stop thinking about creating an environment until we could really work off subtext with each other. When Alexis moved out of the country, Rachel and I would run similar exercises and have set warm-ups so we didn't have to think too much.

In Project2 there are three of us. When we aren't using a coach, we each own an hour of rehearsal with clear outcomes for each exercise so that any one of us can direct the scene. Between rehearsals we'll watch a video of the last show (or just think back if we don't have one) and make notes on stuff we can work on. In rehearsal we'll pick things to work on that have come up. Sometimes we'll gift one another with something we've learned from an external teacher in the meantime. We like to discuss what our intentions were during a show or rehearsal. That means saying stuff like: "When I moved over there my intention was to edit." Rather than blame someone for not getting the intention. Every choice is right, but it is useful to know what the other person was going for so that you become more in tune.

Warming up as a group

As a group, figure out how much you all like warming up. Bill Arnett had The Maydays turn away from one another in a circle and vote by a show of fingers on how much we liked warming up. A vote of one to five, with one: "I hate warming up", and five: "All the time, please." All ten of us were all twos and threes so we did twenty to thirty minutes of warm-ups and then got into scenes and forms after that. Check in with the rest of the group to see what your preferences are. It also depends what you're doing improv for. It might be a nice hobby to get you out of your work head and your favourite thing is fun warm-ups. In that case: go for it. You might have done improv for years and take scenework and shows very seriously. In that case, get into the headspace quickly and start playing those scenes. Neither is better or worse, just make sure everyone is happy. I find that I'm great in daytime rehearsals; I can get right into it, but if I'm rehearsing in the evening I need a good long time to return to an improv mindset, or to change from one type of improv – such as a corporate show, shortform or musical – to another.

Warming up solo

Which warm-ups do you need? If you've been working at a desk all day and everyone else in your group is a dancer, you'll need to warm your body up even though they might not. Perhaps everyone else came from playing another show, but you need a minute to warm your brain up. Make sure as well as warming up with the group that you're personally ready to go. I've had a few shows where I haven't felt connected, silly or physically warm enough before going on stage. Now I just mention that and suggest we do another warm-up for my benefit, or I'll do one by myself.

How to Rehearse Solo

Plan your solo rehearsals ahead of time. Decide which warm-ups you will do, which exercises or scenes you will do and set an alarm for the length of each of these. If you have the discipline to do these without a timer, you are a better human than me. Without this structure, I will make a lot of tea and then hate myself. Give yourself a director alter ego who makes these plans. Film your rehearsals if you like, but remember to be kind to yourself; only take general notes that are positive choices you can make in future, not lines you 'should' have said.

Ask other people to come in at least from time to time so that you have an outside eye. That doesn't mean you have to take on any thoughts or criticism that they give you, but if something rings true it might help your work.

Build in good habits. My friend Dan Attfield puts on a particular music track when he showers every day so that by the time he's got out of the shower he has already done a battle rap. That's five minutes more than no rehearsal without really thinking about it. The aforementioned Brian Jim O'Connell suggests doing five to ten minutes a day of solo improv (whether or not your show is solo). More time than that means you are likely to skive on it. We would all go to the gym more if it was just for five minutes. Brian also suggests that first thing in the morning or last thing at night is the best time. He feels like his brain keeps doing improv overnight and therefore he gets an extra eight hours in every day!

Boundaries and Foundries

Boundaries

It sounds like a simple and obvious thing to have a discussion with your group about what you are physically comfortable with on stage, but it's more rare and more complicated than you would think. Perhaps it seems awkward if you are a new group and trust has yet to be built. Perhaps you feel like it seems braver and cooler to have very few physical boundaries as that seems in keeping with pushing through the fear and doing it anyway? In scripted work, these discussions come up naturally when the director is setting the scene, but we never know what is going to occur in improv.

For a while I imagined that a good basis for people's boundaries were the 'swimsuit areas' and that is a good assumption to start with. But then I discovered what my own were and I became sensitive to those of others. For a start, there is no one map of our bodies that means comfort and discomfort in any situation; of course not. We have people we're intimate with and people whom we find creepy and that will still be true in improvisation. I am happy with any of my regular teams touching my chest on stage if it seems funny or relevant at the time. I don't feel comfortable with anyone grabbing me in the groin. I have individuals that I'm okay with spanking or touching my butt on stage, I feel awkward if anyone else initiates fucking me from behind on stage, but okay if I initiate it. I discovered a few years ago – in a show – that I was hellishly uncomfortable with a team member grabbing me by the hair on stage. He said afterwards that he was trying to make me actually look shocked and scared, but what really happened was that I totally lost the scene because I was just wondering what was going on and feeling horribly uncomfortable. We discussed this as a group a few years after he had moved away but three months later the same thing happened to me with a different member of my team. I felt moderately betrayed as well as physically uncomfortable because we'd talked about it, but of course he had just forgotten. He wasn't trying to shock or surprise me, but create some physical comedy with a dead cow! It's good to keep these chats going, both as a reminder and because people's boundaries constantly change.

I was talking to a fellow improviser on a train journey and she said that she had felt very uncomfortable when a trusted teammate had slapped her in the face in a show. The thing was, we both felt too awkward to bring those things up. It seemed like a whinge and like something that would destroy trust with our regular groups. Of course, the opposite is true. I would definitely want to know if I had overstepped the line with someone else, even if it was a cringey conversation. You can always update your comfort and discomfort with everyone you play with. I did a teacher show at Camp Improv Utopia East in Pennsylvania and discussing your boundaries was secondary only to knowing one another's names before we went on stage. It was like "Hi, I'm Mike, I don't want anyone I don't know touching my privates on stage", "Hi, I'm Katy, don't grab my hair, butt or groin", "Hi, I'm Alice, I don't mind anything" and so forth. I felt no judgment about how big or small the asks were, but instead logged them to myself.

I feel differently in a jam than I do with my regular playing buddies. If I haven't met you, I don't think you have permission to touch intimate areas and I would presume the same about you. Jams are the worst for that kind of thing. New people are in a vulnerable position where they have recently learned the very literal version of 'yes, and' and feel that they should say yes to anything, even if it's miming giving someone a blow job when they're not happy doing that. Dick move (literally) from that improviser asking for that in a jam, but still, it happens. This is really up to the show's host to initiate that discussion before the show starts and to announce to the players and the audience (normally one and the same) what the house rules are. If people are drunk, that's going to make it harder to be aware of what people are comfortable with, so it's best to set a booze limit for performers. I want to point out – though I hope it's obvious – that women are not the only victims and men are not the only perpetrators of negative boundary-breaking. I had a friend who stopped doing improv very early on because he kept being in scenes where women would make him a sexual object and often touch his arse or even groin. Kissing is also a discussion that's important to have especially with your regular teams. I discovered after years with one company that one of us was not comfortable with it. It was actually because his wife disliked it and so he didn't want to upset her. Her view was "I don't have a job where I can randomly kiss people, so why should you be allowed?"

I do a few shows with my husband (*Countdown to Doom*, the *Destination Podcast Live* and *At Home with Katy and Tony*). It's a joy to play with him, but even we had to have boundary discussions! The Living Room is a very confessional show, so we decided beforehand what we were both comfortable discussing about our lives and sex. We also did a *Destination Live* show where he – completely out of habit – put his hand on my arse offstage. I was really thrown by it. We were not doing a scene but on the sides of the stage with microphones. There was a weird crashing together of our home and on stage life that I felt weird about. So we have a different kind of boundary discussion. We are completely comfortable touching one another everywhere, but what is okay in front of an audience?

The main thing is to have an ongoing open discussion and an agreement that it's okay to mention things after the fact. If you run or take part in jam nights, make sure that the stage is safe for new and seasoned players alike by laying out the rules.

Here is a space for you to write down a list of today's boundaries that you have for your own body.

Colouring exercise one!

Draw a picture of the outline of your figure below. Colour in the places where you are happy to be touched with one colour and those that you aren't with another. Write notes around it that include anything else you don't want; like for me, grabbing me by the hair.

Solo boundaries

It may seem odd to talk about boundaries for solo performers, but I'm going to. The boundaries for you are how much of yourself you are willing to show on stage. No matter how close to yourself you play on stage, you are still projecting a persona. What do you want that persona to be? In your introduction you are likely to be most like yourself; before you adopt characters and perform scenes. Choose what you are happy revealing. Do you want to mention friends and family? Are you happy talking about your kids/husband/wife/partner on stage? Are they happy with that?

But mostly, your boundaries should be where this show stops and starts. It's difficult going solo. From my stand-up and solo theatre work as well as coaching solo improvisers I know that it's easy getting the 'you' on stage and the 'you' offstage mixed up. It's very important that you remember that this is your *Act* and not *You*. If it goes great, that doesn't mean you're great, if it goes to shit, that doesn't mean you're shit. So give yourself a sensible rehearsal and feedback process where you can berate or congratulate yourself at particular times and work on your show accordingly. Get a show 'costume', even if that's just jeans and a shirt that you exclusively wear for this show. Delineating this as a show will keep you sane. Make sure that you give yourself space and time to warm up, even if that just means locking yourself in a toilet cubicle beforehand for a stretch and a word-association game. Also, give yourself treats. You deserve it.

Write down your solo boundaries.

Foundries

iO Chicago improviser Jorin Garguilo gave The Maydays a really positive spin on what we are physically comfortable with. Yes, it's essential to communicate what we don't want, but what do we enjoy? Let's do the exercise he gave to us.

Exercise

Get everyone in your group to write down a list of fun things they like being given on stage. It might look like this:

> I like being picked up.
> I like other people initiating.
> I like being endowed with a ridiculous character.
> I like scenes having space and silence.
> I like playing objects.

And so forth.

Everyone should choose one thing off their list to tell the group. Now play a set bearing all of these in mind. It's not a tick-list where all you need to think about is achieving every one of these things for everyone else, but more like a soft goal where you might find yourself on stage with one of the group and think: "Ah yes, I'll make that happen for her." The delightful thing that happened for me, is that not only did I enjoy the set more than usual because I got to do what I loved, but I suddenly had new choices pop into my head because I wanted to facilitate the fun stuff for everyone else.

In Jorin's rehearsal with The Maydays I started a scene with Lloydie, whom I knew wanted to be able to discuss his real life on stage. I set it in a restaurant with me being his best mate who'd stepped in when he got stood up, giving him space to talk about his (real) love life. Liz entered to pour wine and I knew she wanted to be picked up, so I created some business with the wine that meant I needed to lift her up to help uncork the bottle. It's unlikely I would have initiated either of those things without our chat beforehand and we all enjoyed the shit out of that set.

Project2 used to set missions before the show such as 'Make Jon laugh', 'Create cool settings' or 'Do slow-burn scenes'. We would hear all of them, then all agree to have all of them in our heads and that would influence the style of the show in a way that suited all of us. After Jorin's workshop we made our missions things that we personally wanted. There's a fun brain-change from 'Make Jon laugh' to 'I want you guys to make me laugh' or from 'Create cool settings' to 'Give me a brilliant backdrop'. We do this before every show. Don't feel like you have to change your missions every time; it's whatever excites you that day.

Colouring exercise two!

Illustrate your list of fun things you'd like to be given on the picture from colouring exercise one above. If you love being picked up, draw someone picking you up. If you love someone endowing you, have a speech bubble coming out of the other character's mouth and so on.

The idea is not to limit your physicality and interaction with the other players of course, it is to make it safe. Improvisers build trust through stage time and rehearsal and that includes physical trust. Enjoy interacting, touching and being vocal about what you love and what you don't.

I Need a Hero

I'm teaching at the sixth Maydays Improv Retreat (MIR) festival in Dorset. I teach several days a week in London, but there is definitely something unique about MIR. I love to be out in the sticks, walking to my class across dewy grass, past last night's still-smouldering bonfire and always a short walk from a privet maze.

At MIR, every class needs to be self-contained so that – like a Choose Your Own Adventure book – students can take any journey through the program and it will still make sense. Big group warm-ups happen at the start of the day, so each ninety-minute class gets right down to it straight away.

On Thursday I offered a class that I hoped would equip the students for the rest of their time at MIR. Students are sometimes in a class with people who have a very different style to them or have a lot less/more experience. I decided that the best thing to teach was a toolbox of ways to deal with that gap.

'I Need a Hero' is the name of my class. It's the first time I've taught it and it's a bit of an experiment. We start by playing some group story games, doing scenes where the crazy person is a genius and overagreeing with everything because everything is brilliant. We're enjoying it, but I'm suddenly worried that I don't know where I'm going with this. What's the big headline for this class? Everyone knows that they need to support the other person; that's all improv *is*, right?

We try some scenes where one person does whatever they want and their scene partner tries to make them look great. It's hard work. One of my class asks a question. Apparently someone in their troupe bulldozes them all the time. They talk over the other players and push their own ideas all the way through the scene. I have someone play the Bulldozer and we work out some solutions and tactics. They're bulldozing because they're scared, because they don't trust you. Reassure them, mirror and have a high-energy scene. It works. I learn stuff too. Another hand goes up. "There's someone in my troupe who hardly says anything", "I work with a guy whose body is totally closed off", "This girl always plays negative". We keep on like this. "What do I do when I get denied?" Justify. "What do I do when I'm getting nothing back?" Make nice big inclusive offers. "How do I stop this one girl walking through my furniture?" Put your set somewhere that doesn't interrupt the whole stage/make her a ghost or a hologram/make sure she sees what you're doing.

I realise the point of my own class. It's not about *tactics*; it's about respect and trust. It's not *dealing with inexperienced improvisers*, it's that every offer your scene partner makes is the right one. Rather than being annoyed that a total beginner stepped into your scene, you get to practise even harder at being the best support in the world. If you handle it that way, they will look great, like a genius. If they do the same for you, improv is the best art form in the world.

As I'm walking over the dewy grass to join the dinner queue (still smiling about some of the scenes), I realise that my class was doing for me exactly what I was trying to teach them: support. I wanted to offer them a way of helping their buddy, I got lost and they just showed me what they wanted to learn. I needed a hero and we made each other look like geniuses.

Get the Most Out of a Workshop or Coach

How to choose

It's important to find the right coach. I've had some excellent coaches who didn't work well with the show or the company and some fairly average coaches who still happened to be the right person at the right time. I've also found the perfect coach for one thing or another and they click the show (or company) into place.

Find someone whom you like to watch or play with on stage. Do you want to do that kind of work? It's important that you don't all get taught how to improvise like them, but rather use their insight to become your own improviser. If you trust them and in rehearsal you're having a good time, feeling like you're pushing yourself and doing good work, that's your coach. You may want to change them up every so often and learn from as many places as you can to make sure you're rounded.

Whenever I have a new coach or go to a workshop, I am exposed to the Hawthorne Effect: even though I try and be honest about how I improvise so they can help me improve, I am modifying my behaviour because I know I am being studied. Even if I fight it, there's still a 'teacher's pet' part of me that wants to be liked and praised. I'm a girl, society has raised me to be perfect or not bother. But like taking the pressure of a tyre, you must let the air out of it in order to see how much air is in it. We must make mistakes on stage and in our classes in order to get pumped up to the right pressure.

In my first iO intensive workshop in Chicago I was told to play more women by one teacher, the next week I was told to play more men. I was new and therefore frustrated that I was getting contradictory notes, but of course, they could only comment on what they saw. More experienced me understands that I need to try and do my regular work in a class in order to be assessed in a way that's helpful.

In a workshop I will try and put a wide range of characters and energies out there, I will try and initiate as much as I follow and balance my work out. It might even be misleading because I'm probably not as balanced when I perform, but it's good for my muscle memory to be the most supportive team player offstage so that I can try and bring that on with me when my ego wakes up to the spotlight.

When you get individual feedback from a teacher, those notes are not limited to the ten minutes they're focusing on you. You can be working those muscles for the whole rest of the class, or in your head when you're watching someone else's show. When I'm working on something, I find it freeing to do it every other scene rather than every single one. It's like taking a break between reps and it keeps the skills you're comfortable with up to scratch too. That was a piece of advice from Annoyance's Mick Napier.

Take notes

I take notes even if I'm getting a handout or email at the end of the day. The stuff we write down is the stuff that gets through to us as individuals. You can't write everything down and please don't miss anything because you're tucked away in Notes Land, but having notes is like being able to repeat the workshop whenever you want. I still take notes on paper so that I have to type them up. Typing them up reminds me what we did and gives me time to reflect and relearn. Repeating (and teaching) the exercises soon after also helps me get the most out of it.

Take the note

COACH: "You were talking a lot in that scene and could have done less work by listening to your scene partner and building on that information."

IMPROVISER: "Yeah, I just didn't really know where we were, so I thought it was best to build a platform so that we were both on the same page. I don't normally do that."

I've been guilty of not taking a note, but defending myself. I often see fellow players do it when we're in a class, being coached or directed, and I see it in my students too. The coach (let's use that as a catchall for teacher/coach/director) tells you something that you did and you – however subtly – argue with them.

Our art form is built on 'listening', 'yes, and' and 'commitment'; use those tools in your process as well as your art.

Take the note.

When I was studying at iO Chicago in 2008 I had a class with Jet Eveleth where we were playing scenes in which our emotions started at one and went up to ten throughout the scene. We chose an emotion beforehand. I remember choosing fear and Jet misread it as anger. She was coaching me hard on the side to get more angry when I was confused because my choice was fear. I was torn; do I do what she says or what is true to the scene? I hated my scene. I felt awful and I was annoyed at her for not listening to me. I wasn't taking the note. The note – intended or not – was that the portrayal of my emotional choice was not clear early on. It didn't matter whether she chose the wrong emotion or not, I was at fault. Instead of learning, my ego was bruised and I probably wasted some class time talking about it.

I heard a nice acting note that I sadly can't remember the origin of and it's also true for improv. If you find yourself saying "My character wouldn't do that" then *find* a reason why they would. If you normally wouldn't play an improv scene like this, find a reason why you should.

- The coach already knows you weren't doing it on purpose; you don't have to assure them that you're normally better than this.
- If it's a behaviour you didn't know you have, you should listen rather than question whether it's true.
- You waste group time by having a big conversation about it.
- Stop protecting your ego and learn to fail. Failing is how we learn to be better.
- You are paying for opinions, don't hand them back.
- Giving an excuse is a way of protecting yourself and stopping criticism from getting to you, but if you stop it getting to you, you aren't going to change your behaviour.
- You don't need to apologise. You are learning and that's the whole point.
- If it's the first time you've done this or the thousandth time, it doesn't matter. That note is there for the next time; to stop you falling into that trap again.

- It's unlikely to be a judgement on you, but on your work. Make sure you can separate the two.

If you really don't agree with the coach, that is fine. However, rehearsal is not the time for that. Take the note on right now and use it hard at least until the end of your rehearsal. Even try it out in shows and if it's not useful or not a fit for you, you can discard it later.

Hooray! You've made it to the end of Week Two.
Let's go through our weekly practice checklist.

Read

Did you read the chapter? Hope so!

Improvise

Here are a few games that you can play right away so that you're touching one another!

CALIGULA

This is a game I learned at iO; I think it came from Susan Messing. Here everyone holds hands in a circle, then they move in a beautiful way where each person maintains contact with at least two people the whole time. It doesn't just need to be hand-holding, it can any point of contact. Keep moving and have fun, see where your body wants to go. It makes for a great abstract image and builds up physical trust.

TWISTER

This game has evolved from a Project2 rehearsal. Jon was in charge of an hour or so where his remit was 'Project2 get physical with one another'. He wasn't sure what to do, so he just brought a game of Twister along. I totally stole this for my twoprov classes and got people to have object work mats with voice-activated spinners (the spinner is the dial you spin that tells you where to put your feet and hands on the coloured dots of the Twister mat, e.g. "right hand blue"). I'm assuming you've played Twister. If not, get the real game! With a made-up board, you can start to put yourself in trouble. Make terrible decisions about where to put your hands and feet; get nasty and close and enjoy the discomfort! The game ends when one or more of you falls over.

MOUNTAIN CLIMBING

My actor friend Dan Starkey described this to me in the pub and Project2 tried it the next day. We imagined that the floor was a vertical cliff face and all three of us climbed it to get to a ledge higher up. We attempted to balance on each other (on the floor), hoist one another up and so forth. It's very fun. It's also silly and comedy when one of you falls to the bottom. Now I've put this game into my coaching, I enjoy noticing when the moves completely defy gravity!

Watch

Did you manage to see a show?

What was it?

Reflect

Write down your notes or thoughts on what you read, saw or did this week.

Week Three:
You and
Your Characters

It's not just what we decide to play on stage – but whom. Having a clear character choice can make scenes run along by themselves: we sometimes feel that we are 'channelling' a character when they flow so effortlessly from us. When you know exactly how they will respond to any impetus, characters are a dream to play. Some people prefer to play characters that are close to themselves and others prefer to get inside the skin of very different people. In this chapter we'll look at both approaches for creating and playing in scenes.

Inside-Out, Outside-In

Character is a combination of characterisation and point of view; that is your outer life as a character and your inner life too. Some people find it much easier starting with the characterisation of the character; working outside-in. Those players are often those that lead with emotion and physicality in the natural way they play. Others will find deducing or creating a point of view and working inside-out much easier. They will tend to be thinky or writer types.

Characterisation

If you walk around the room imagining that you have a rope pulling you forward from one part of your body, it changes your body shape, your rhythm and your way of walking. It is sometimes called 'stacking' as you're stacking your spine into a different position to alter your stance.

If you change your voice – the pitch, the accent, the rhythm of it – what kind of person do you become? If you start with physicality as above, what voice would suit that person? If you like doing accents, can you play five different people with an accent from the same place? All Welsh people have different voices, so challenge yourself not to just do one Welsh guy, but lots of Welsh people.

You could also put one (ridiculous) facial expression into play and try and do a whole scene using that expression. It's something your character is used to, so they're not going to comment on why their face is like this.

These three affectations are like a chicken-wire mesh that we can use to build a character on.

Point of view

If you start with the point of view of a character, the physicality will follow.

I learned some great point-of-view stuff from Rich Talarico. We played objects in a room, just sitting on chairs, so there was no staging or much physicality. By talking to the other objects, we found out what our point of view was. I was surprised and delighted to discover that this came out organically. It was clunky at first, but soon I found that it was clear how much the old clock envied the new side table or the fireplace fancied the lamp.

Now the BEST PART was then giving someone else your role in this scene. We would pass them a card that said 'lamp' or whatever we were playing, but explained to them who the character was as if they were our understudy. The clearest character explanation ever. It's not about the text of the scene, it's not about the accent or physicality because that's up to the actor herself. It's a clear point of view. "You are really trying to please the cabinet, undermine the fireplace and be one of the gang." It's not that different than having a secret want or motivation or goal, but it's about the other characters in the scene and your attitude towards them.

Next the characterisation comes into play. How would Disney or Pixar play a lamp? What voice would this one have, how would it stand or move?

Explore outside-in or inside-out depending what comes naturally and then work on the one that comes less naturally to broaden out your range.

Making Characters

As well as looking at whether you start externally or internally on your characters, here are some approaches to creating new ones.

Emulate

Ronnie Barker was a comedian whom I loved when I was growing up. He had so much range. He could play big, ridiculous characters in a sketch show, or well-studied real-world people that seemed to have a rich inner life. In order to find new characters quickly for repertory theatre, or for *The Two Ronnies* sketch show, he would do impressions of famous people. Ronnie admits that he was terrible at impressions, but that meant that he would come out with a new character. No one would recognise the source for that persona, but he would have a quick way of getting into their physicality and point of view because they were fully formed in his mind. I love this idea. I also love to play people that I know. They don't know I'm doing it; I'll change names and specifics, but it's a great way of thinking less and just playing.

Observe

TJ and Dave recommend watching people. Rachel Blackman and I adopted this a few times and we would sit around doing the voices of people we could see in public, imagining their worlds. I have days when I am just collecting characters on my travels. I stop reading or listening to podcasts on public transport to see and hear people. How do they walk? What do they sound like? Who do I think they are? It's these characters that would have audiences coming up to us after shows and saying, "Oh my God, that character was just like my friend!"

Thin veil

You may have heard this phrase being used in improv. It means playing a character that is very similar to yourself. Some people are more comfortable playing in this way and others feel too exposed and like to use the shield of character to protect themselves. In order to play this way, I use my opinions and experiences to start, then surrender them to the scene. When something no longer rings true to the scene, I make another choice that feels right. For example, "I love the countryside, but I'd go crazy if I lived there" (which is true). My partner might set the scene in a country cottage we were looking at and then I would be playing someone finding it difficult to move to the countryside.

Add depth

We have built-in stereotypes to our culture but it's not always a smart way to play. If you find that you're doing something super-broad – for example, if you are a man using a high-pitched voice to play a woman on stage or having your point of view being penny-pinching with a Scottish accent – people may be offended, but also, you're not doing anything new. If you find yourself in that corner, try and collect other dimensions for that persona as you play the scene. Does penny-pinching Scottish guy want to save all that money to give to charity when he dies? Does high-pitched woman enjoy track days in an Audi? If we just push back a little bit against what we imagine to be the well-trodden route, we may find an individual from the pool of well-known types.

As always, there's a caveat: if you're playing in a specific genre, stereotypes are your friend. Even then, take the John Hughes approach and let us find out something new about the Jock and the Nerd. Outwardly that's what we get, but they are richly human too.

From genre

Even if you're not playing in a genre show, you can take characters from different worlds into any scene. Decide to play someone from a Western before you go on stage. This will give you a voice, physicality and a point of view straight away. Now plug this person into the scene. If your scene partner is in a Shoreditch café and your character is their friend, you don't need to tell them about your cowboy past, just play through the choice you made. It might mean you pick fights with people, that you're pretty quiet, that you don't trust anyone, that you like to lean on things and walk deliberately and that you drink your espresso like a shot of sipping whisky. Just start with the genre and let the scene determine your new context.

Mirroring

A great way to get a brand-new character for yourself is just to copy the one your scene partner is doing! It often makes for great agreement and 'peas in a pod' scenes. You aren't the same person, but you probably have the same physicality, the same view and the same emotional standpoint on a lot of things. You can also try playing this character 'better' than your scene partner, by which I mean streamlining their opinions or heightening what they brought. If you're both heightening, it's going to be a fun comedy scene. Look for phrases or sounds that you share as they may end up being buttons for laughs!

Impressions

You could be in a scene where you think it would be a good move to play a famous person or you might be endowed to be a celebrity or politician. You may or may not be good at impressions and you may not even know who they are! Not knowing feels difficult and in this case you may worry that you really could get it wrong. The wisdom I got from Jason Chin was to play whichever figure you need to as truthfully as you can. If you were in this position, how would you react? Impressions are often a distraction from the emotional life of a politician scene anyway, so be you as if you *were* the Prime Minister or President and react in a human way. If you're doing an impression of a person who exists, the audience are likely assessing how good or bad that is, rather than caring about the content of the scene. If you're amazing at it, or really bad, perhaps that's entertaining enough, but I'd go with emotional honesty every time.

Personal prop

Remember the volleyball in *Cast Away*, the watch in *Pulp Fiction*, the pill in *The Matrix* or the ring in *Lord of the Rings*? They are all pretty mundane objects that have been given huge importance by the people interacting with them. Giving yourself a mimed prop that is important to your character really helps you get a clear point of view and gives you ideas about who you might be. I end up playing characters who smoke a lot in improv shows, but I try to do it differently with every smoking character I play. Try not to let your personal prop drive the story. Frodo's personal and emotional struggle translates better to improvisation than us all needing a payoff at Mount Doom.

As you can see, there are a huge number of ways to get into character.

Bring Yourself to the Stage

Truth in Comedy (by Charna Halpern, Del Close and Kim 'Howard' Johnson) was the first improvisation book I ever read. Truth is something amazing and interesting that sets good comedy and theatre apart from shallower work. It's also the driving force behind a lot of improv philosophies. Let's talk more about playing a 'thin veil' of you and address why that scares some people a little.

When I started doing stand-up comedy, I was a little too scared just to stand up there and talk about me. I didn't think I'd be interesting or funny enough. That's how some people feel about improvising either as themselves or in telling monologues. My way around it was to play comedy songs all the way through my set. I could hide behind my ukulele and the lyrics were set in stone. People rarely heckle in songs. As my confidence grew, I would play less music and the links between the songs would get longer. I actively enjoyed being heckled because it allowed me to respond and improvise. I would find a lot of good material by talking to the audience. It turns out I did have interesting and funny things to say.

Sometimes we try so hard to be experts in things we don't know in improv, we forget that it's okay to be an expert about things we do know. Doctors can play doctors on stage; pilots can play pilots and cleaners, cleaners. We only care about the specifics being there, we don't mind if they're made up or real. The effect is very similar.

Here's an account of a Katy and Rach show I did around five years ago:

"We never know what's going to happen in Katy and Rach and it's always a joy to find out. We met early at our venue The Miller on Wednesday, where director Alexis Gallagher took us through his genius warm-ups. We had a fairly small crowd, but though The Miller was only half-full, the audience was warm, enthused and loved the show. With some eye contact and the position of my hands, we found we had started Katy and Rach with a little improvised close-up magic. The show became about magicians, the Magic Circle, and the hell of children's parties. I'm a big fan of object work in improv and had a ball playing Ian, pillar of the Magic Circle whose whole career revolved around his cane tricks. The favourite of these was turning his cane into his business card. The audience actually gasped as if it was a real magic trick! I love improv. People really join you with their imagination.

There was a crazy point in the show when Rachel's character 'Park of Darkness' (yes, that was her name) was attempting to go into trance for a séance but couldn't. She asked her geeky boyfriend Mark to help out. At this point – as Mark – all I could think of to do was to cast a magick circle. A real one. As a dabbling pagan I know how to make a sacred space by tracing the outline and invoking the quarters. It felt odd to use lines I know, but if you were a real vicar who ended up playing a vicar in an improv show, you would totally use scripture. I realised at the end of the show that I hadn't closed the circle, so I asked the producer Steve Roe if he wanted me to take it down. He decided he was cool with leaving it there for a couple of weeks and then we'd use the power that had built up in the circle to do some improv good. I also met a man at the end of the show who claimed to be the Druid Mayor of London and he loved the show! Brilliant."

We care about people because of their stories. We do the Armando and the Living Room as longform formats because we want to know about the people playing in the show. We want to see the human condition and relate other people to ourselves.

What Are Your Superpowers?

I can't remember who gave me the analogy, but I really enjoyed being told that an improv teacher is like Professor X (Charles Xavier) attempting to train the powers of his students.

This analogy is lovely because it underlines the fact that we are all individuals. There are a lot of improv schools around the world with house styles, and students learn the ropes and fit in with that way of playing. You'll often see improvisers, however, who seem to defy the rules or the house style while still standing out as being successful as well as supportive.

I'd like to unlock your superpower, but first, you'll need to study others.

Write down your top ten improvisers in no particular order (the ones that you love to watch):

Write down your top ten improvisers to play with, in no particular order (ones you have already been in scenes with):

Now have a think about the superpowers they have. Are they all technical improvisers? Do they all play game hard? Do they all play big, fun characters? Do they all make big emotional choices? What do they have in common?

Write down one thing that stands out for each of your favourites.

For example:

1. He's so fun-loving.
2. She completely inhabits a character.
3. They listen to every detail.
4. When he reacts, he reacts big.
5. He plays women very well.
6. She is excellent at picking language apart.
7. He takes his time.
8. They step right over boundaries with a lot of energy.
9. She has great sketch-like scene ideas.
10. They are both casual and emotional.

For the next week, pick one of your top ten improvisers (to watch) and attempt to play as they would, in any rehearsals and shows that you can. Even if you're practising solo, choose which player you will emulate before you start. Try on different ones in different rehearsals and shows.

Report back

How does this influence how you play? My favourite improvisers make big, stupid choices and those are justified by those around them. However, when I play on stage, I feel like I'm not allowed to be the one to do that. I don't want to make the improvisers around me have to be the caretaker of my weird stuff, so I become the caretaker for them, which I enjoy a lot less. So I will be the stupid one, making stupid choices for my next rehearsal.

Whoo-hoo! You've made it to the end of Week Three.

Let's go through our weekly practice checklist.

Read

Did you read the chapter? Hope so!

Improvise

Here are this week's exercises.

Trade superpowers with your team

Ask yourself what are three things that characterise your improv?

- I make the scene science-fiction.
- I play word games.
- I climb on people.

Now ask the other members of your team to list the three things they do most.

Jen says she:

- Plays old women with northern accents.
- Uses specificity and detail.
- Follows rather than initiates.

So I will take Jen's ways of playing and just use them for a while and she will have mine. You could also write everyone's three things on paper and pick them out at random (as long as you swap if you get yours). After trying on the styles and go-tos of other improvisers – those you know and those you just watch – you'll notice more about how *you* play. What did you enjoy about seeing your top three when other people were trying them out? What didn't you enjoy? Ask other people what they think your strengths are. What do you do really, really well that is perhaps harder for other improvisers?

My superpower is:

```
┌ ─ ─ ─ ─ ─ ─ ─ ─ ─ ─ ─ ─ ─ ─ ─ ─ ─ ─ ─ ─ ─ ─ ┐
│                                               │
│                                               │
│                                               │
│                                               │
└ ─ ─ ─ ─ ─ ─ ─ ─ ─ ─ ─ ─ ─ ─ ─ ─ ─ ─ ─ ─ ─ ─ ┘
```

With a bit of variation in your style, you'll be able to choose *when* to use your powers rather than them being your regular fallback. Doing your special move in Street Fighter is all very well, but sometimes a well-timed punch or duck is more useful than a spinning bird kick.

You will also find that your superpower will change over time, so pop back to this exercise in a year and see what has changed. Who are your heroes now? What do you do better than before?

Exercise

Pick five or more actions from the following list. You can choose the ones you like the most, choose the ones you are most scared of in order to push yourself or write them all on paper and pick some out at random.

- Choose one body part to lead with, allowing it to change your physicality.
- Adopt a weird facial expression and try to hold onto it throughout the scene.
- Try out a brand-new voice in a scene or monologue.
- Pick strong points of view towards the other characters on stage.
- Emulate someone you know.
- Allocate one hour to people-watching, even if it's just taking out your headphones or putting your book away on public transport.
- Initiate with an opinion that you really hold.
- Start by playing a stereotype in a scene and add depth.
- Pick a character from any genre and take them into a scene.
- Mirror and heighten the character your partner has chosen to play.
- Play someone famous as if they were you.
- Pick a personal (mimed) prop and let that inform your character.

Group exercises

Cocktail Party (I learned this from iO)

Get six of your team up on stage, sitting on chairs as if they were three couples at a restaurant. Give the first pair a topic to talk about like 'holidays' or 'pets' or 'superheroes'. Have that pair talk about the topic as themselves. They are not playing a character, they are not trying to be funny, they are only saying things that are true. If they know nothing about the topic, this time they do not need to pretend they do. Each person in the pair should do around the same amount of speaking. Rather than asking a lot of questions about the other person's opinion, bring your own to the discussion.

Was it interesting? Were there points where the audience laughed? Did you find it hard to be truthful? Did you bail out by doing 'gags'?

Now give the next couple a topic to talk about and repeat for the third pair.

In my experience, each of the conversations will be funny and revealing and entertaining. You'll notice that if the actors revert to 'trying' to entertain, we lose our connection with them.

Now have the conversations (the same three topics they started on) edit themselves from one to the other using a line they just heard. If I heard 'I hate the way I have to travel' in holidays and my conversation is 'pets' I will repeat 'I hate the way I have to travel' and finish it with 'to the vet'. As if there were one microphone on a boom, the sound comes up on one conversation at a time, passed back and forth by repeated lines.

We have an improv scene created totally by truth using a high level of listening skills. I bet you can also see larger themes developing across the independent topics too.

Some more ways to bring truth to your scenes:
- Try initiating with a truth about yourself. "I didn't get my period until I was fourteen."
- Try reacting as *you* would when presented with a line of dialogue.
- If you're in a scene with an improviser you've never met before, treat them as if they were your best friend.
- Play the character of your dad.

MONOLOGUES

Try using your real opinions and anecdotes to improvise a monologue. Here are some tips:
- The longer the silence, the bigger the expectation; it's easier just to start talking and trust your brain to provide.
- Show your working, e.g. "Hedgehogs make me think of…"
- Stand still (your story will wander if you do).
- Don't look at your feet.

> "The ground is where we bury dead people. Don't look there for ideas."
> Brian Jim O'Connell

Monologues for improvisation are mostly used as an opening or game beat of a show. They are the scrapheap from which we pull useful and valuable materials to make scenes. Monologues are not stand-up comedy and there is no expectation for them to be funny. They will be interesting as long as they are true and personal because humans are interested in other humans.

As you monologise, ask yourself:
- What does this say about me? "I guess this means I'm the kind of person who derives energy from other people."
- What does this say about the world or people in general? "I suppose people are still interested in connecting with strangers."

- You don't need to provide comedy ideas for your team during your monologue
  – they will find them in whatever you say.
- Be honest. The audience can smell bullshit from a mile away.

Watch

Did you manage to see a show?

What was it?

Reflect

Write down your notes or thoughts on what you read, saw or did this week.

Week Four: Editing and Openings

This chapter is all about beginnings and endings. Starting scenes and shows well helps the show as a whole and gives you an easier time on stage. A well-placed edit can turn a less successful scene into an excellent one. We'll look at different types of edit, what to do if you feel stuck at the start of a scene and how to step up if you're worried about editing or make more generous choices if you have a short fuse for editing.

Editing

Editing in longform is the act of finishing or cutting away from one scene and/or starting another. There are lots of different ways to edit and it's also fine to create your own. The most commonly used and universal ones in longform are the Sweep and the Tag.

Sweep

Run across the front of the action to sweep the stage clean of action. The editor can join the next scene or continue across to the far side as other actors fill the space. A sweep should immediately be replaced with another scene so no empty stage is left. I've also seen a lot of editors raise their hand like a shark fin as they cross, which seems unnecessary. For me, an edit should be fairly invisible to the audience. We're not broadcasting to the audience that we're editing, we are telling the other performers. Let's make it look like a beautiful, choreographed move from one scene to the next.

Example:

Scene 1

>   DAVE: "...thanks very much, I hope we meet again soon."

An improviser who is not in this scene runs across the front. All improvisers in the scene leave the scene and go to the side of the stage. One or more improvisers enter the stage at the same time to start a new scene.

Scene 2

>   WENDY: "...I just think sewing is one of the most relaxing things I've ever done."

Tag-out

There are a few different conventions to a tag-out, so here's the first version I learned. If you tap someone on the shoulder, they leave the scene and you enter it. The result is that you are left with one or more original character(s) on stage. It means you can transport a character/characters to another time and – optionally – place. Outside of a two-person show, it can get confusing to an audience if we're sharing a character, so you are not replacing the character you tagged out with the same character, you are playing someone else. The person you tagged out is looking for the first opportunity to tag you out and resume the original scene. Tag-outs are normally to illustrate something that has come up in the scene. They should add information rather than just playing something out that we already know, unless it's something we'd really like to see.

Example:

Stephen is talking to Mike.

> STEPHEN: "Judy was such a kind and loving girlfriend."

The actor playing Mike is touched on the shoulder. He leaves the stage and is replaced by the actor who tagged him. This actor plays Judy.

> JUDY: "You're a total shit, Stephen, I don't know why I wasted my twenties on you."

'Mike' tags back in and 'Judy' leaves.

> MIKE: "I wonder if her beauty somewhat eclipsed her personality."

It's like a quick cutaway and cut-back in *Scrubs*, *The Simpsons* or *Family Guy*. If you have an idea or inclination to do a whole scene, don't use a tag-out to do that. Keep the idea and use it a few scenes later. That is, unless you're doing a form where the convention is that tag-outs move from one scene to another.

You can also use tag-outs to move from one scene to another. This convention is used throughout the Slacker form as the only edit following any character to another time and/or place.

Tag run

A tag run means that one person is tagged out, but rather than coming back to the original scene, another actor will tag the person who tagged in. This way we can get a lot of quick-fire examples of something.

This example happened in our Living Room show *At Home With Katy and Tony*. One of the performers says in his story: "I mean, who rings your doorbell at midnight?!"

An actor initiates a scene where they are ringing a doorbell. The door is answered.

| PAUL: | "Hello?" |
| PIZZA GUY: | "Hi, here's your pizza." |

Pizza Guy is tagged out. Doorbell.

| NEIGHBOUR: | "Can you keep the noise down? Our kids are trying to sleep." |

Neighbour is tagged out. Doorbell.

| FAIRY GODMOTHER: | "Your pumpkin is here, sweetie! Run!" |

And so forth until we get a really good laugh or go as far as we can. The game of this tag run is to illustrate occasions when someone might ring the doorbell at midnight. In a different scene you might have ten examples of patients who have been given bad advice by their doctor ("So you think praying will help?"), ways that someone was bullied, historical taglines for cigarettes or whatever you like. You can also set up the other person in the scene to deliver the punchlines. If they have declared that they get really annoyed at tiny things, you can just keep coming on with examples of insignificant things they can react off ("Ah nuts, I broke a nail").

Object edit

You can take an object that has been established in the scene before and bring it into a new scene. It could be narrative like a cursed lamp affecting various different families throughout the show. It could be used purely as a physical or thematic link where you take an apple from scene to scene. You could also take the object and morph it into something new for the next scene; then it's a physical handover and perhaps a way of changing pace.

Crossfade

A crossfade is simply one scene starting without the other stopping first. You might begin a scene in front of one that is happening. We might hear a few lines from each before the original scene ends and those earlier actors leave the stage.

Split scene

This is where the scene is broken open as if the audience have both A and B cameras. For example, two actors face front during a transaction over a counter, one hands money out towards the fourth wall, the other actor takes it from in front of herself. They talk, react and 'touch' as if they were standing in front of one another. You could use this with one looking up and one looking down as if one was in a well and the other above.

Split screen

This is where you might have two totally different locations seen on stage at the same time. It's very like a split scene, but instead of cutting between viewpoints, we are cutting between scenes. A group of men might be on one side of the stage getting ready to go out and on the other side, a group of women might be waiting for them at a pub. We can pass the focus back and forth either with a soft freeze of the action in one place, or we mime talking as the sound is taken up by the other side.

Baton-passing

I made up this term, but it's something I saw in a TJ and Dave show. In many of their two-person shows, they moved to new sets of characters by meeting a new person every so often. It went something like this:

Two people are chatting in a car and they pull in at a drive-through. One of the actors plays the server and the other stays in the car, still talking to their (invisible) friend. The actor in the car then moves to play the other waiter. The car drives off and only the servers remain. A new car pulls up. One of the waiters becomes a cop from the car, the other joins them. We follow the car and leave the waiters behind. They go to a video store, one of the actors plays a member of staff, the other becomes another customer… and so forth. We can make a circle of this as a show format by the original couple coming back.

Montreal edit

I call this a Montreal edit, because I saw it done by Marc Rowland and Brent Skagford from Montreal. I've also heard it called a French edit. Imperceptibly, a new scene starts! We don't see an ending and a beginning as with most other edits. It is immediate. One actor will just change. It might be something they say that doesn't fit with the current scene, and/or the character they are playing is suddenly different. This cues the other actor that the scene has changed. There is no big physical change as part of the edit.

Swarm

A swarm is an organic type of edit where an action or mention in the scene inspires a physical choice. One actor will start with sound and motion and the rest of the group will join in. The group will enter the stage, consume the actors who will also join in, then leave behind the actors for the next scene as they exit. For example, an old couple might be reminiscing about the seaside trip they once took. An actor may choose to be a seagull. A group of seagulls will emerge, the couple will join in. The seagulls swoop and caw and then leave the stage so that two or more actors are left behind to start a new scene.

Organic

This is very much like a swarm, but it is often more abstract and the scene following the edit will be inspired by the energy or physicality of the edit itself.

Patterns of editing/game of the show

If you have done a particular type of edit in the first few scenes of a show, this is now in your hands for the rest of the show. Perhaps you sang a song while you edited? Repeating a style of edit and themes from the show can be your way of moving from one scene to another. Now every edit involves singing a song and it doesn't have to be you that does it because that edit belongs to your lexicon for this show now. Make the edits as important as the scenes themselves.

The timing of edits

It seems odd to talk about editing in an art form where we make everything up as we go along. Yet, editing as we go along can make or break a show. If scenes are too short we might miss out on emotional depth or they might never find their feet. If they are too long, a joke might fall flat or the actors might have to work really hard to maintain interest. The timing of an edit can characterise the show itself. If you choose to edit on your very first impulse then it's usually on a laugh or on the who, what, where being established. Quick edits in the many shows I have seen tend to support a comedy show. We have an idea or context and a laugh and that's it. Reframes and gags are okay, because we're not worried about destroying the integrity of the scene. The whole point of the scene was to get a laugh; we got one, move on.

Rachel Blackman and I have scenes at the top of our forty-five to sixty-minute show that last twenty minutes, or sometimes the whole show will be a monoscene. We like to edit when we have explored the characters we started with.

I asked a group to edit on the very first opportunity they saw. We had a lot of punchy, fun scenes, but we didn't get a lot of character depth. Next we tried to edit on the second opportunity; so they would watch the first edit go by and look for the next. On the second edit, the scene ended on a laugh, a point of intrigue or after the game had been found/made. Next I asked them to edit on the 'third' edit; whatever that felt like to them. That means counting off on your fingers the first two good times to edit and acting on the third. This led to deeper character scenes with good subtext, properly established game play and sometimes a rescue because the air had gone out of the scene and it needed an earlier edit! We discussed how each of these felt. This team was smaller than they had been in the past and were finding that they were losing performance energy in the show. Spending a bit of time on the rhythm of edits broke patterns they had established when there were more of them. The exercise is quite a good spring-clean for an experienced group and a great way of finding your tone if you're new, even if you're a solo performer.

Much of the time, the group had similar ideas about what the first, second and third edit points were. Discussing them is a great way of getting to know the group mind of your team. Try running some scenes with everyone – apart from the players – raising their hands when they would edit. Only move to a new scene when everyone has their hand up. You can discover through discussion what the successful edit points are for the show you are trying to achieve. Having a coach or director in rehearsal is very useful for this as you can all have different opinions on the subject and someone can make the ultimate decision.

There are often groups in which the same one or two people are doing all the edits. That person may feel like everyone else is dropping the ball, but perhaps those fast edits are ahead of the feeling of the group.

I was in a group where I initiated lots because to my mind the stage was empty for too long and I felt I had to fill it. Later I discovered that others were annoyed that I would initiate so much. I just thought: "Then why the fuck don't you initiate more?" They told me they didn't feel there was space. So I hung back against my instincts until others got a bit more experience and confidence at coming in first. We establish these habits, rhythms and patterns with our teams sometimes without noticing until they're ingrained. Keep changing up the edits, the pacing and the regular roles you fulfil in your team.

Jurassic Park III

I am lounging in Café Adonis on a sunny day at the Barcelona Improv Festival. There is a family sitting opposite me with an attractive couple and their child excitedly drawing his parents on a huge piece of paper. I am drinking a No. 6 Green Tea and aching a little from the hostel bunk bed I've been drunkenly sleeping on. I love to go to international improv festivals because they are a top-up for the improviser's brain. Our troupes, our countries and our brains get too settled in one way of playing, or at least in a series of patterns.

I played in a 'mixer' team last night (where people from lots of different groups and countries play together for perhaps the first time) and there was a lot of open space on the stage where people feared coming on. In fact, the last scene was me filling an empty stage (despite being on perhaps too much in the show already) as the Deputy Stage Manager signalled for us to end the show. No one joined me for the bow, so a new scene gradually emerged with other improvisers joining the stage to me shouting and gesturing: "Come on, guys!" My point is GET ON STAGE and don't leave your team hanging.

I was teaching longform at Hoopla recently and was reminded of the tiny movement I often see out of the corner of my eye. It means someone at the side of the stage has an idea. It happens in almost all longform classes (and a lot of shows). It's not even a whole step. It's often an intake of breath, a tensed calf or a list forward. Students are sometimes surprised when I say: "You have an idea, go do it," as if their bodies hadn't betrayed their thoughts.

> Doctor Grant: "I have a theory that there are two kinds of boys. There are those that want to be astronomers, and those that want to be astronauts. The astronomer, or the palaeontologist, gets to study these amazing things from a place of complete safety."

Erik: "But then you never get to go into space."
Doctor Grant: "Exactly. That's the difference between imagining and seeing: to be able to touch them."

When those students are on the side of the stage, they are astronomers and palaeontologists; they get to see the history of the universe in the scenes of the other players. It's hypnotic and it's beautiful. It's a discovery. It can feel active because you're making deductions; finding out how, who and why, but if you don't follow your feet, then you never get to go into space. When you do have that idea or you just need to fill the space and support someone: go!

Become an astronaut.

Doctor Grant: "And that's... that's all that Billy wanted."
[A *field of beautiful dinosaurs comes into view.*]

Dialogue from *Jurassic Park III*

Help! My Scene isn't Working...

Sometimes in an improv show we find ourselves in a bad scene. How on earth do we deal with that?

Trust that your team will edit you

They should know you well enough to feel when you're uncomfortable, or understand improv well enough to know the scene isn't working that well. They will edit the scene, just like you would do for them.

Stick with it

Okay, so no one edited you. Shit. Ah, man, now you're up in your head. What do you do? The first thing is, don't edit yourself. It can be very tempting but it will look like you are bailing on the scene (which you are). By making an excuse to leave as your character, you are leaving the other actor(s) high and dry. By editing the scene itself from inside, you are not trusting your team to edit at a good time. We have other people edit because we are bad judges of the scene we are in. There's a lot going on in our heads, so it's best to let the rest of the crew take care of that while you stay present in the scene.

Eye contact

So no one's editing you and it's bad practice to edit yourself. It doesn't help being up in your head, but since you're there already, let's use your brain to help you. Your scene partner has everything you need. Look them in the eye. What is the emotion that's coming across? How do they feel about you? It may be that we're both thinking ahead and forgot to connect. We can build this show together.

What you just said is very important to me because...

Listen to the last thing your partner said. What were the exact words? Why is that important? Forget the rest of the scene for now, what did they just say? Now decide why that's so important to your character. Why is this thing so important to me? It works for any line. If they say: "Peanuts are shitty," what they just said is very important to you because you also think peanuts are shitty and the amount you have in common suggests they would be a great life-partner.

Have an emotional reaction

It's great saying that something is important to you, but the best way to telegraph it is to have an emotional reaction. If knowing your relationship is going really well makes you feel good, show that. It also helps your scene partner react off of you.

Say what you're thinking

Can't decide on an emotional reaction? Say exactly what's happening in your head right now.

> "I can't do this."
> "Why is no one helping me?"
> "I can't wait till this is over."
> "What's wrong with me, I could do this yesterday!"

These are all really great offers for your co-pilot. Don't break the fourth wall by commentating on the scene, e.g. "This scene is shit." Say how you feel as if it was happening to this character in thi moment. "I feel like I've forgotten how to do this." It helps you be authentic while also giving your fellow improviser something to play with.

Build a platform/define the who, what and where

If you're feeling lost, see if there's anything that hasn't been defined. Knowing who you are to the other player(s), where you are and what's going on is really helpful. You don't always have to do these things in the first few lines, but if you're unsure, setting up the pieces will help you play the scene.

Slow down

Some shows can get very information-heavy with full and complicated plots and/ or lots of characters. If you don't quite know what's going on in the show or in the scene you're in, take a second. Some people's coping mechanism with a fast-paced, complicated show is to add more information. If you're talking over one another, trying to solve a story by putting more facts in there or adding something different because you don't want to contradict what's already happened, just breathe. You don't have to be talking all the time.

So, let me just get this straight...

If you're not sure what's going on, there's a good chance that at least some of your fellow players and the audience will be lost too. Try saying: "So, let me just get this straight..." and outline what's going on as best you can. You will clarify what it is for yourself, your team and the audience. If you've massively misunderstood something, great: you'll probably get a laugh and someone will fill you in with the 'correct' information or justify your mistake.

Use your environment

What if the problem is that nothing is happening? What if you're just a rabbit staring into the headlights of the audience? What if no one joined you on stage yet? Discover your environment. Perhaps you know where you are and perhaps you don't. If you don't, make a decision. It doesn't matter where you decide to be; make that decision and stick to it. Now reach out and touch something that would likely be in that environment and use it. For example, if you push a button, it might tell you that you are on a spaceship!

How you do what you do is who you are

The way you use objects and environment gives you clues about your character and emotional state. You picked up an apple. Did you peel it with a knife, did you break it in half with your bare hands (as my mum used to do) or did you bite into it? What are the clues you get from these decisions? Are you aggressive, are you smug, are you considered? Whatever it is, use it to form your character and emotional choice for this scene.

Don't drop your shit

Great. You know what's going on, you have made a connection with your partner, you've made a character and emotional choice. Now stick with it. You don't have to keep thinking about whether or not they were good choices, you just have to double down on them. Escalate the shit out of them.

Be changed

But... if your scene partner offers you something that might change your outlook or your emotional state, use it. It's a great gift. Allow your peanut-hating old man to fall in love, despite his reservations and his penchant for carrying an apple knife.

Now they edit you

And you feel pretty good about it.

Suggestions and Going Lateral

There are a few schools of thought on how and what suggestion(s) one should get from the audience in order to begin an improv show. Some believe that you should take the very first thing you hear to prove to the audience that you're improvising; you're not seen to choose and there is very little time to plan. The thing is, after a certain amount of shows, there is only so much inspiration you can glean from "dildo", "spatula" and "under the sea". I used to argue that it was important to take the first suggestion and that it was a challenge to do something interesting with it, even if it was "brothel" for the four-hundredth time. The performers being delighted and inspired by the suggestion makes for a better show.

One way of getting better suggestions is to burn through the ones you hear all the time in your introduction. "Please can we get a suggestion of a location that would fit on this stage" (which stops people just shouting out a country) "like a bowling alley, moon-base or playground?" Please don't use the phrase "non-geographical location". No one knows what the hell that means and you will lose half the audience. Everyone I've seen doing this always has to qualify the phrase with a suggested location, so just say "like a café" in the first place. Try not to use improv speak to an audience that will undoubtedly have at least some element of newcomers to the art.

Whether you like the challenge of taking the very first call-out or you like to choose or vote for the best, it doesn't really matter so long as you and your group feel good about it. I was once in a show where the host didn't like the call-out and just announced her own, "Desert Camp". Despite the fact that I didn't know that was going to happen, I felt like a total cheat and didn't like that we were doing something that looked pre-planned. Also, it was aggressive because the audience had shouted locations and she just didn't like them! If something is pre-planned/written then it has a totally different audience expectation around it; it needs to be more polished and none of the crazy bits that make improv fun will be forgiven. However, if the host had said: "We are going to set an improvised show in a Desert Camp, please can I have a suggestion of an object you might find there?", I (and the audience) would have been totally fine with it.

113

In terms of using the suggestion, I like to see scenes that are a little lateral. Ninety per cent of beach scenes I have witnessed start with a couple on the beach and one of them awkwardly applies suntan lotion to the other. Sure, that's the most obvious place our minds go but that's also where the audience's minds go. We haven't achieved anything new or different and it's going to take work to be inspired by this starting point. It's true that the location doesn't matter when you find good game or relationship, but why work so hard when you can be excited right away? What other connections do you have with beaches? Have you walked the dog along a pebble beach in the winter, have you been a lifeguard on a tower, have you gone fishing for mackerel, have you gone skinny-dipping in the moonlight? Okay, so I lived in the beach city of Brighton for nine years, but there are more imaginative places to start your scene. It's not always summer and you're not always sunbathing with your partner on the beach.

Sometimes you will be given a suggestion word from the audience and you won't know the meaning. You have a couple of options. You can take it anyway and explore what it sounds like to you or you can ask the person who suggested it for clarification. There's no need to apologise for this. It's a nice moment of truth and communication with your audience. I am a fan of asking for "a word you have learned recently". That way I'm likely to get a suggestion I've never had before and I'll create audience rapport as I ask them what it means. I'm expanding my vocabulary too!

As well as your suggestion (if you take one), you will have a first scene or section of your show. These are some classic openings for your show:

- Monologue or shared monologue: One or more of the cast tell a true story (or discuss an idea/opinion) based on the suggestion.
- Character monologue(s): Characters speak to the audience or to an imaginary other character.
- Conversation: The cast talk about the suggestion.
- Word association: The cast perform a structured word-association game.
- Invocation: A description and thematic elevation of a given object. See Del Close's format for this.

- Organic opening: Often an abstract three-chapter physical exploration of the audience suggestion with some words.
- Scene-painting a location.
- One slower, broader scene.

Kudos! You've made it to the end of Week Four. Let's go through our weekly practice checklist.

Read

Did you read the chapter? Looks like it!

Improvise

Here are this week's exercises.

ONE AND THREE

Run a bunch of scenes. Raise your hand when you see an edit.

1. Edit on the first opportunity.
2. Edit on the third opportunity.
3. Edit on the best moment for the type of scene that is happening.
4. Edit at the best moment to support the variation of scene length in the show.

FUN WITH EDITS

Try all of the edits in this chapter, whether you've done them before or not.

NEW EDITS

1. Run a (say twenty-minute) longform set with your team or on your own. Write down all the types of edit you used in that set.
2. Now do another set where you are banned from using the edits you tried last time.
3. Repeat this a few more times until you are forced to create new ways of moving from one scene to another.

LATERAL SCENES

Write a list of ten locations you have seen or played in more than once. For example:

1. Under the sea
2. A castle
3. Sainsbury's supermarket
4. A restaurant
5. A classroom
6. Army training camp
7. Yoga class
8. The beach
9. Behind the bike sheds
10. A brothel (ugh)

Pick the top three; the ones that you have seen or been in the most. Now play three scenes in each of those locations. Make the first one the most obvious scene you can set in that place. Give the next two a new approach.

For example:

'The beach'

1. A couple on holiday (obvious).
2. Litter-pickers the day after a music festival.
3. Archaeologists looking for fossilised dinosaur footprints.

'A brothel'

1. Two women talking about sex (obvious).
2. Two women working on the accounts for the business.
3. A painter and decorator agreeing on design with the Madam.

'Behind the bike sheds'

1. Two teenagers smoking (obvious).
2. Two teachers hiding from their lessons.
3. Two monsters waiting to pounce on kids.

Your location:

1 (obvious).

2.

3.

You can rehearse this with any call-out. Get into the habit of thinking a little more laterally. You are still doing what the audience asks of you, but you are also surprising them.

118

Watch

Did you manage to see a show?

What was it?

Reflect

Write down your notes or thoughts on what you read, saw or did this week.

Week Five:
Theatre

This week is all about the theatre. In improvisation we have props, scenery and costume, but most of the time they are imagined with the use of language and object work. We can also borrow a lot from the theatre to make our art form more watchable; raising our skills in stagecraft and acting.

Theatre

Improv is largely about the suspension of disbelief. If we hold the audience's attention in longform, we can take them with us wherever we go. How can we create comedy or straight theatre through improv that hooks the audience as deeply as a well-written and well-acted play?

Improvisation has its roots in *Commedia dell'Arte*. My favourite story about improvisation was told to me by my university lecturer, John Harris. The story goes that an Italian theatre group had a famous *Commedia dell'Arte* player in their audience one night. They did not believe that her shows were as improvised as they were purported to be, so they put her to the test. They pretended a member of their company was ill and asked if there was anyone in the house that could help out. She offered to step in. They told her the broad strokes of their scenari and she improvised the whole thing. Apparently, it was the best show they ever did.

With our skills, we get to be her. I was once due to go and see Music Box perform and they needed someone to step in. I had never played with them and improvised a one-hour musical at short notice. Perhaps our training holds more in common with a team sport because our rehearsals are for raising skills and practising forms – and our performances are all very different. You might know the rules of football, but you won't know what this particular game looks like until it's over.

Sometimes theatre is a friend of improvisation and sometimes it can be the enemy. We (mostly) create objects, costume and set on the spot because the real things – although they lend a sense of legitimacy – will narrow our universe. Is it better with those things, or without? This is an area where there are a hundred answers and you just need to pick the one that feels right for you and your show.

I think there are broadly two types of shows; one that gives you actual props, costumes, set and a narrator or director to steer the show. It holds the player's hand and does the imagining for the audience. The second is visually neutral and minimal so that it can go absolutely anywhere and the imagination of the crowd is a big part of the show. The improv itself is steered by the whole group, not one person, so that you are not distanced by one authorial voice. If you are doing a genre like musical theatre, Jane Austen, Shakespeare or science fiction, having a visual hook such as Empire-line dresses or sci-fi overalls may help your audience get on board. If you want to have the world at your fingertips and the audience's imagination as your prop store, then object work, scene-painting and character specifics can give you everything.

Props

Object work or space work is what improvisers call the mime they do in their shows. Mime is a misleading term because it conjures up images of street artists wearing stripes and walking into the wind. In longform, we might play big, like street-theatre clowns, or use objects just as we would in real life. The latter is my favourite, even in a wacky universe or with science-fiction props.

When I first saw the two-man improv show *TJ and Dave*, I remembered it as if it were a film. Their object work was amazing; I could tell which notes and coins were going in the till and which sweets were where in the DVD rental store. (The what store? Don't worry about it.) Object work is a skill that's worth spending time on. Specifics are incredibly useful in improv. The audience love it when you agree physically about where things are and what things feel like, just as they do when you agree verbally.

I have been on tour with character, storyline and theme-driven improv company Fluxx. It was the first improv company I worked with where we'd use physical props. At first I found it very difficult because my choice was hugely narrowed down from 'anything' to 'these things'. This worked in a different way, meaning that the choices were made for me and the audience were easily on board with anything I used. I had a scene where I took a pack of cards on stage. I played Snap with another character and it was perfect that he won the game. It would have been perfect the other way too and the show would just have changed direction. For performers and audience members, real props make for a very accessible form of improv.

Personally, I'll always be married to object work over actual objects. When you're specific enough, there are a lot of beautiful moments that come out of it. Project2 had a show where the first second or so saw us run to an escape pod and me shut the door before Jon was inside. Not a word had been spoken, but the audience laughed a lot and Jon and I had found our points of view already. I was specific enough about the escape-pod door that Jon knew what it was and what it meant to be locked out of it.

Objects not only set the stage, they give clues about the time period, character status, the occasion around the characters and the characters themselves. If you're stuck for someone to be, take a look at what is in your hand. A pipe is going to give you a very different character than a fan or a tiny dog.

Some people find object work the most natural thing in the world and others find it very hard, but it is something you can learn and practise. Try the following:

Give everything weight and depth

That means leaving space between your fingers (hands, knees, hip and forearm…) to allow for the object, even if it's something really thin, like a comb. Move it as you would for real. Don't wave that drink around or talk while you're pouring it in your mouth; we won't believe you. If you're carrying something heavy, we want to see that your muscles are engaged.

Make clear decisions about the object

Don't just pick up a drink; pick up a square, weighted glass of freezer-cold Icelandic Reyka vodka over ice. Swill it gently as you improvise, switch hands or put it down because it's so cold. The firmness when you put it on the table will be palpable. A square, heavy glass is very different from a champagne flute and if you have physically decided what drink it is, the audience will come on the imagined journey with you.

Don't use real objects (unless that's what you have decided to do for the whole show)

You may feel like you want to pull out your actual phone, or that tenner you have in your pocket, or take off the jumper that you're wearing. All of those things are fine until the phone needs to get smashed, the note should get eaten or the best move would be to take the rest of your clothes off. Object work means that there's no real limit to the things we can touch and how we can use them.

Object permanence

Make sure the object continues to exist when you are not concentrating on it. If you forget to make space for the object in your hand, it looks to the audience like you have dropped it or it will seem like it is appearing and disappearing. It's very satisfying when more than one improviser uses the same prop. Going back to our drink – the most common of mimed objects – having one person set their drink down on a chair and another pick it up seems incredible to the audience who notice it. Conversely, someone sitting on that glass and nobody mentioning it will distract many of the audience from the scene altogether. Let object permanence be at play in your shows.

Move things when the other improviser is looking

Perhaps that sounds obvious but there have been dozens of times when I've seen an improviser 'secretly' steal or move an object behind their scene partner's back. It might be a lovely plot point but if the actor doesn't know you're doing it, they can't help you. They have no idea you made an offer and the likely outcome is that they will contradict it by picking the thing up that is no longer there, or they'll simply be unaware and the offer will be dropped. Make that offer in their eye-line, however, and the improviser can decide whether their character has seen it or not.

Your hand is not an object

Using your thumb and pinkie as a telephone, drinking out of your thumb with your closed fingers as a bottle or using your forefinger as the barrel of a gun are all super-weird! I suppose these gestures are echoes of theatre shorthand, but they look really strange when everything else is mimed like reality.

Mirrors are fun

I'm always satisfied when improvisers are talking while looking at each other in the hairdressers' mirror or the driver is talking to her passenger via the rear-view mirror. It makes it easier for the audience to be transported into that world without thinking about it.

Scenery

Your audience are ridiculously suggestible. If you tell them what is on stage, they will see it in their mind's eye. There are lots of ways of creating scenery and world-building in improv.

Object work

Which you know all about.

Character dialogue

When characters use their improvised text to describe their surroundings.

> "Oh Peter, this sunset is delightful! Look at the way the clouds have gone pink."

Scene-painting to set the stage

An actor who is not a character in the scene walks on and describes the environment as a narrator would.

> "There is an empty old bookshelf at the front of the stage with rectangular gaps in the dust where novels once were."

Build the scene together as a group with one aspect of the space described at a time by different players. Keep to a small number of things so that the actors get to be in the moment rather than playing a memory game.

Bring chairs!

If you scene-paint anything that could be sat on – like a sofa, a chair or a stool – it is the job of your team to bring a chair (or two or three) to that spot while you're describing it.

Scene-painting during a scene

If one character was boasting about all the awards they had, a scene-painter could walk on and say: "There are half-a-dozen rosettes in a glass case, all of which say 'for taking part'." Therefore giving the improviser a clue that their character was someone who exaggerated, or who was proud of every little thing they did. *Or* the scene-painter could describe a 200m vault lined with golden awards, and the character would be elevated. Your job is not to tell the whole story in your scene-paint, let that unfold collaboratively. It feels odd at first to interrupt the scene; do it confidently and speak to the audience. The actors can be in a soft freeze (which means not frozen, but also not going on with the action) or carry on with the scene without dialogue while you scene-paint. The actors shouldn't look at the scene-painter because the scene-painter does not exist to the characters.

Use your senses

You can describe more than the visual aspects of your scenery. Set the scene with the sweet scent of roses, the hot damp atmosphere, the buzzing of cicadas or the choking taste of petrol in the air. If you talk about something you can touch, put your hands on it to help the audience and the improvisers see exactly where it is. Gesturing isn't quite as useful or satisfying. When you touch it, react to the touch. For example: "This velvet feels exquisite."

'Yes-and' what is already there

A room with a rubber diving suit, a bible and a teapot might sound fun, but it means that you're asking your improvisers to make sense of a weird trio, rather than giving them somewhere fun to play. Having things that naturally live together is another way of 'yes-and'ing the reality. Put that rubber diving suit with a harpoon and a map of the ocean and we are providing the backdrop for a scene that agrees with itself. The actors get to make the scene about one another rather than justifying the setting.

Make it easier for others to live in your world

Improvisers often walk through imagined furniture or set pieces. Make sure bars, tables, cars and so forth are generated in full view of everyone. As insurance, it's great practice to put the big things in the audience. You need to make a bed? Put most of that bed where the audience are and just tuck in the corners at the front of the stage; it's going to be very hard for someone to walk through it and you will still get to have a bed.

The audience likes to see your face

It feels natural to put bookshelves, pictures, mirrors and such against the back wall. That's where the actual wall is, so it makes sense to us. However, the staging is better ninety-nine per cent of the time if you put it against the fourth wall, the wall that doesn't exist between you and the audience. That way we get to see what's going on with your character while you're stacking books, looking in a mirror or admiring a picture.

Be objects, animals and extras

Rather than physically or verbally describing things, you can just be them. To make a glade in the woods, a group of improvisers can embody a backdrop of trees and animals. Actors love to play trees. Try being other people in the background of a scene like playing extras in a movie. Be the creepy family portraits in a haunted house, the food at a buffet table or the animals at the zoo. Remember to listen to the scene when you're being background and keep your voice low or mime speaking. I sometimes get very excited about being a squirrel to the point where I forget to take in the scene that is happening. If you're being an extra or part of a backdrop, don't upstage the characters that are the focus in the scene. That's part of 'making the other player look good'.

Costume

What should you wear to improvise? The cliché is to wear Converse, jeans and a check shirt. It's not a bad thing, because it means that you're wearing something relatively neutral that you can move around in easily. It's also wise to look smart, because it adds legitimacy to our art form and makes the audience feel better about paying for a ticket.

Teams sometimes choose company colours or a T-shirt with their logo. In genre shows pick something you would expect to see in that genre. Whatever you choose will make the audience form an opinion. What impression do you want to give? What is the feel or the style of your show?

Avoid anything too revealing, which might include low-cut tops, shorts where we see your junk when you sit down, dresses and skirts without thick tights or leggings, or old jeans that have worn out in the crotch. I'm saying this not to sound like your mum but because these things distract the audience from the great work you're doing in your scene. I find myself doing handstands, performing dance moves, being animals, having sex and a million other physical abominations. If you're doing that kind of thing and you're wearing something revealing, people won't notice how hilarious or heartfelt that scene is. The problem sits with the beholder, I'm sure, but we are still stuck with the (fe)male gaze. I suppose there's an argument for "Wear whatever you want" and screw the gaze, but personally it distracts me and I'd rather watch the scene.

Freedom of movement is important too. I find it restrictive to improvise in heels, but if you can run, climb and crawl in them, that's fine. Hooray for the invention of stretchy jeans.

Your face is your best conveyor of emotion and a great tool for getting laughs, so try not to hide your expressions with your hair, a hat or a pair of glasses. I do wear glasses in shows but I'm switching more and more to contact lenses. Glasses not only partially hide some of your expressions but in a physical show, you may lose or destroy them! They have flown off my head a few times over the years.

Project2 wear science-fiction costumes, but like everything that is solid, it does alter the content of the shows. We started by wearing overalls customised with patches from all of our favourite science-fiction franchises. We thought that was quite a neutral choice for a costume. It allowed movement and gave the impression of science fiction in general. What actually happened is that we spent the first three years playing a LOT of engineers on spaceships. The thing is, even if you're trying to be neutral, what you're wearing will influence your style. In the end, we switched to plain black costumes. Jon's is a shirt, tie, trousers and long coat with echoes of *Blade Runner*. Chris has ripped jeans, a tunic top and a scarf, which gives the desert feel of *Star Wars*. I have a denim one-piece which does 'space adventure' pretty broadly. I can be a captain or a cleaner or a bug or a queen in that outfit without it being too much of a stretch.

Suspension of Disbelief

If your show is enthralling enough, the audience will willingly enter into the unreality that you present to them. I want to suspend my disbelief but there are some things within improv that can throw me out of a show. Let's look at the grey areas of laughing, meta jokes and kissing.

Laughing

Do you laugh while you're improvising in front of an audience? It's also called corpsing or breaking. Many improvisers break into uncontrollable laughter on stage and some ask me if I have any tips on how to stop it happening. But *should* we stop corpsing?

We laugh for lots of reasons – because something is funny, because it's a surprise, because we're scared or because we're uncomfortable. Sometimes that laughter becomes irrepressible and then we're into corpsing territory. Improv is the perfect petri dish for this kind of laughter; we're constantly being funny and surprising and putting ourselves in scary new territory. The immediate reaction of most people to laughing in a scene in class is that they apologise and try and get back to the scene without laughing. I personally think it's fine to laugh, but it's all about how you use it.

Laugh all you want in shortform. There are buttons for laughter built into those games and the audience enjoy the Brechtian angle of seeing both the actor and the character. Theatresports and Comedy Sportz also have actors pretending to compete – in which case we enjoy them laughing to show us that winning is unimportant.

In shows with a fourth wall, laughter can compromise a scene if you let it become corpsing. It takes the audience out of the immersive feel of the show, reminding us that these are performers playing characters. Ergo we care less about the emotional journeys of those characters.

Laughing in and of itself is not actually the problem. Say you're having a scene in which some bad news is imparted. If one of you corpses and then tries – as yourself – to cover it up, you have lost the audience's belief; if you treat that as a genuine character reaction awesome. That's a great choice to have made and comes from truth, so it can really help your scene. I see a lot of scenes where improvisers play upset – crying even – but far fewer where the characters themselves are laughing out loud. What a beautiful gift.

What about being on the other side? What do you do when your scene partner breaks? If someone other than you laughs, double down on your character and react how they would react in that situation. See how much more fun it is than breaking the moment. Committing to that isn't the boring, 'supposed to' route; it is the more fun, deeper-end route to making great improv.

As well as breaking the dramatic tension of a show, laughter can sometimes feel self-indulgent and alienating for an audience. If you faux-corpse, I reckon everyone sees right through it. It reads as a cry for attention and a way of telling us that you aren't confident enough about your show.

> "I'm going to laugh to show you all what a good time I should be having but I am cold inside."
> Jorin Garguilo

Like any rule or guideline, some companies just get away with breaking this one. A small percentage of performers demonstrate their joy at where they are and what's happening to such a delightful degree that all of the above is forgiven. With those happy few, I can continue to care about the characters, not be annoyed by a smugness at their own performance and actually have a better time. Perhaps the difference is that those people are enjoying the improv of their fellow cast, they're not worried about the show and they really are just... laughing.

Meta

Meta means being self-referential, like calling out that you're in an improv show.

> "Well, this scene is weird."

I'd much rather believe what's going on and enjoy what's happening with the characters. Meta choices can come out of fear and a desperate need for a laugh and are often characterised by improvisers pointing out 'errors' themselves or their fellow performers have committed.

> "I thought your name was Jane before?"

It will likely get a laugh, but the actors will have to work harder to make anyone in the audience care about any of the characters now that the audience's willing suspension of disbelief has been shattered.

I am bored by how many times I've seen someone correct themselves or someone else on their accent: "So where are you from exactly?", "What is that accent?" When inconsistencies happen, they are the ultimate gift for your show. If a character has been given two names, justify the reason for that. Are they undercover? Are they in a witness-protection programme? Do they like being called by their middle name? If an accent is strange and unbelievable, make up a place that it comes from or agree with any country that was already stated. Making your scene partner look good means using these moments for good and not evil. Your choice might be getting a quick laugh for yourself or saving someone else's error to keep the scene intact. There are different choices here depending on the show you want to make, but I know that I'd rather someone make use of an error to add to the reality rather than shatter it. There was a moment in a Dasariski show where a couple of the cast were making the sound of a helicopter by slapping their chests. They paused at one point because it was exhausting. The characters in the helicopter panicked beautifully and realistically crash-landed. The bail-out version would have been a "I guess the blades have stopped working" wink to the audience and we wouldn't have cared about those characters.

Kissing

In a scripted show, the writer has decided that these characters will kiss, so the actors do it. In an improvised show, the actors are writing the show as they go along, so there's some odd self-interest at play in the pleasure (or discomfort) of kissing. Watching, I always wonder whether the improvisers are loving or hating that moment. How can we stop kissing from bursting the bubble? The only thing to do is for the moment to be played truthfully.

You will already know the boundaries of the people you are playing with, so you'll know whether kissing is on the table. If not, job done; it won't come up or you will be swiftly edited. There is a responsibility for the improvisers offstage during these moments to edit the show where it has the most power. Tune in to what seems okay for your fellow performers so that they always feel safe to explore these moments. They will save you before it goes too far, or they will make it worse if they know that is okay with you and serves the show!

Jon and I were in a Project2 show and there was a moment where it felt like our characters should kiss. It was an emotionally charged and sexy scene over a birthday cake. What we did instead was bail out of it. Discussing the moment afterwards, we found that we both thought it should happen, but Jon was worried about kissing me and I was worried about it throwing people out of the show. Actually, not kissing threw people out of the show, because it's exactly what needed to happen between those characters. Whether or not Chris edited, we should have honoured that moment. Avoiding a kiss that should happen destroys the moment just as much as kissing when there is no need.

High five! You've made it to the end of Week Five.
Let's go through our weekly practice checklist.

Read

Did you read the chapter? Hope so!

Improvise... like a pro

It's definitely worth spending a lot of time getting really, really good at improv. Those 10,000 hours take a while though, so it's nice to have a couple of tips. My mum always allowed herself 'two cheats' in any board game and I'm generously giving you ten. Watching a lot of new improvisers as I do, I notice the same tells over and over again that broadcast them as such. There's already a lot to think about up there and then there's abandoning all of that to get out of your head; but even if you just work on one of these at a time, you'll come across like a more experienced improviser.

1. Be comfortable in your body

Be purposeful in your movements, even if your purpose is to be a loose, nervous or random character.

Exercise

Practise silent scenes. Not 'gibberish' talk, but scenes that don't require dialogue. You'll be listening much more closely to your body and the bodies of your fellow players.

2. Stagecraft

Take care to make an interesting stage picture and make sure everyone can be seen.

Exercise

Make single objects, animals or machines as a group without talking. Look for symmetry and beauty. Support your team.

3. Straightforward

Be open, honest, real. You will get laughs from authenticity.

Exercise

Play the fifteen-year-old version of you throughout a scene. What would fifteen-year-old you have said and done in this improvised situation?

4. Be heard

Make sure you can be heard. That means enunciating as well as projecting. Be aware of the farthest person at the very back of the room and say everything so that they can hear.

Exercise

Wheel out all those tongue twisters you know. Perform them loudly and confidently with exaggerated mouth movements, imagining you are in a huge theatre. Try "She stood upon the balustraded balcony inexplicably mimicking him hiccupping and amicably welcoming him in."

5. Taboo

There is no pressure on you to create 'shock' laughs. What a lot of people feel is pushing the boundaries of art and being risqué is often just mentioning cancer, rape, paedophilia, racism, scatology or violence. Trust what's already happening in the scene and heighten that. More often than not, you'll find a much more satisfying scene there.

Exercise

MAPPING. As truthfully as you can, act out a scene with a couple breaking up. Now play the same scene again, but make it all about chess instead. See if some of the same phrases will fit ("We just don't play together like we used to"… "Since when have you been playing chess with Charlie?"… "I think I need some space").

6. Variety

Vary your character and emotional choices.

Exercise

EMOTIONAL ROLLERCOASTER. Play a scene as a director calls out different emotional directions for the scene to take.

7. Meta

Stay inside the reality of the scene. It will help the audience come with you.

Exercise

ORDINARY/EXTRAORDINARY. Play a scene as mermaids/ghosts/werewolves, etc., but keep all the dialogue real-world. How would mermaids chat if they were just having a normal day?

8. React

Play a scene where you emotionally react as your character would. Look out for offers that will give you this opportunity and create them for yourself.

Exercise

Have your scene partner reveal a secret and choose a strong emotional reaction (not necessarily the logical one).

9. You're great

Even if it feels like a mistake, make it look good, justify it and sell it.

Exercise

EIGHT THINGS. Get the title of a list and very quickly name eight things on that list (types of fruit, things you find in the sea, etc.). Have everyone cheer at all eight things whether or not they make sense or should be part of that list.

10. They're great

Even if it feels like a mistake, make it look good, justify it and sell it.

Exercise

Be ridiculously excited about everything their character says in a scene. Even if they say "Let's kill her" be really happy about that and tell them why it would be a brilliant idea and how they could do it.

More exercises

The best way to practise is to be mindful when you're touching real objects. How do you type, drink tea, vacuum or read a book? Try putting the real object down and attempt to play through the movements exactly the same way. You'll discover that everything is much more complex than you had first thought. When you're rolling a cigarette, where do you put the filters, the papers, the tobacco and the lighter?

Have one of your group walk onto the stage, pick up an object, use it and put it down again. They leave and another player walks on, interacts with the same object, interacts with a new object and then leaves. Continue this for up to five performers. If you aren't sure what the object is that they have picked up, take your best guess and make your interpretation of it as clear as you can for the next person to touch it.

- Paint a scene prior to the actors entering.
- Paint a scene while the actors are playing.
- Be the scenery.
- Play extras.

The Tube

This is a London-centric exercise that I created for my longform students, so please make it applicable to your local area by using public transport in a similar way. Alternatively you could also choose a park, tourist attraction or pub that has varying patrons and a totally different atmosphere depending on the day or time of year.

Create a physical description of 'the Tube' with everyone playing humans. I'm guessing you will bunch together on a busy carriage and be annoyed with one another. Hopefully you will have synchronised movement and some announcements, each of you finding your own occupation like headphones, a book, a child, etc. Now ask yourself if every Tube train you've been on has been this busy. If you're commuters, the answer might well be yes, but I'll bet there are drunken last trains you've been on, early morning going-to-the-airport trains, Sunday sit-in-the-park-with-friends trains and more. Try and think of another likely time or event that takes place here. For this exercise in London, set the scene for the Tube at different times of the day.

- The Northern line at 8 a.m. (completely jammed, the doors will open, but not everyone will be able to get on. People ignore one another despite being literally in their armpits).
- The Piccadilly line at 6 a.m. (sparse, but full of suitcases and sunhats as a lot of customers are on their way to Heathrow Airport. A lot of these people don't commute, so some are clutching Tube maps, fingering sunglasses and chatting to a travelling buddy).
- The Victoria line at 1 a.m. (full of alcohol-fuelled groups of friends, sometimes singing, sometimes being sick, sometimes getting into arguments).

Have someone start building the scene at a different time/date that only they know. Watch and build on what they bring. For instance, if the first person takes a child onto the train, it's unlikely to be late at night, so it might make sense to bring an elder on, searching for a seat. Build the scene in this way and we find something less clichéd.

Try a few of these, speeding up the entrance of the improvisers without losing the attention paid to the offers of the people before. Now you have a great setting for a scene and you are being physically specific about not only the environment, but the tone of the place and the people in it.

If you need it, here are some tips to stop you corpsing in your improv show:

- Get more stage time. The more you play in front of an audience, the less of an altered state you'll be in when you perform. You won't be as scared or self-conscious and you'll have more control.

- Treat everything that happens as intentional. If you laugh; make it a character choice.

- Play GIVE ME BACK MY SON. I saw Zach Woods play this on *Conan*, it's based on *Ransom* with Mel Gibson. Walk up to someone in the circle and say "Give Me Back My Son" with full commitment. They are not allowed to laugh.

- Play WHISKY MIXER. Stand in a circle. The phrase "Whisky Mixer" is sent around to the left. The direction can be changed by saying "Viscous Mixture" which moves round to the right. You can pass across the circle with "Mister Whiskers". Errors should not be registered at all. There is no laughing or pausing. If you say "Schmictuk Whisk" by mistake, there's no need to correct yourself and then the game continues as if you had it just right. You can play with elimination or people running around the outside of the circle if they laugh.

Watch

Did you manage to see a show?
What was it?

Reflect

Write down your notes or thoughts on what you read, saw or did this week.

Week Six:
You

This week we'll be looking at how you personally improvise. There are different types of improviser that you can both learn to appreciate and break out of. We'll see how you can stretch into areas that come less naturally to you and start to talk about the unhelpful nonsense your inner voice tells you and how to approach your own fears.

What Kind of Improviser Are You?

It's unrealistic to pigeonhole improvisers into one bracket or another, but in planning a rehearsal for The Maydays, I realised that there are things that we get into the habit of practising and avoiding depending on our innate style and on the needs of the groups we play with.

I read a book called *Why Men Don't Listen and Women Can't Read Maps*. It points out that in a romantic relationship, we sometimes work like a two-person ant colony; if one of us can do one job, then there is no point in the other taking up brain space to do it too. One of us learns everyone's names at a party so the other one doesn't bother; one knows how to make the surround sound work so the other one doesn't bother. We have one double-sized brain between us. In an improv troupe, there is something similar. After years of playing with the same people, we can end up having a specific role in our company shows and rehearsals. The positive aspect of this is group mind. The downside is habit and stagnation.

Without really thinking about it, I know that within The Maydays, we have improvisers who are stand-out aces at character, singing, rap, game of the scene, 'follow-me' initiations, object work, clowning, emotion, lateral thinking, topics, support and, of course, cock jokes. Because individuals are so good at their particular forte, sometimes it is easy just to leave it to them. The only reason we don't leave it to them the whole time is because we generally have a cast of four to five per show and our company has twelve improvisers. Each show has a different vibe and we find that there are golden combinations. If you can get good at all the stuff you normally avoid, then when you're in a show where everyone you're on stage with is character-driven, you can be the one remembering names at parties or sorting the surround sound.

To be the best improvisers we can be and to be able to play excellently with improvisers we've hardly even met, we have to have the whole set. If you don't practise all your improv keepy-uppy, you won't be good enough at it when the nerves kick in, when you're under the weather or tired, or when your mind goes blank.

Clown, Thinker or Caretaker

Here's my system that categorises the three main types of improviser.

The Clown

Clowns love to come on stage with a strong character or emotion. They sometimes pull their character idea off the call-out/scene before and sometimes just pick an arbitrary emotion, choose to lead with a certain body part (stacking), or alter their face or voice. They love to sing or rap – and find it easy – because it is a way of channelling their emotions.

Clowns avoid driving the plot of a show or the journey of a scene and they don't like to be the initiator. Their reasoning is often that they aren't 'clever' like that or that they can't think of anything in time. If they do initiate, it is often just an initiation for themselves. They don't want to be in charge of the other improviser and their journey through the scene.

Bad Clowns are particularly scared of initiating and just wait for their scene partner to do the work, partly out of misplaced politeness. The other type of bad clown is someone that will just cock about until they get a laugh. It's often funny, but can end the scene abruptly and make the show pretty shallow. Bad clowns can also get stuck in stereotypes or in their regular go-to characters.

Good Clowns really listen to the show as a whole and allow their rich characters to embody the themes and feelings being tackled. They can change the rhythm of a show and take the audience into deeper states of emotion. Good clowns often get this audience feedback: "Wow, you were just like this person I know."

The Thinker

Thinkers love to initiate and drive scenes and help tell the story of a show. They love to talk. They're very good at conversational topics, verbal games of the scene and reincorporation. They always remember names at parties.

Thinkers avoid playing big characters or characters that are wholly different to themselves. They also don't tend to go for full-on emotional responses or very physical scenes. Their songs will be all about the lyrics, less about the melody.

Bad Thinkers tend to talk about action or plot instead of showing it to us. They get cross when the scene or show isn't panning out how they thought. They fight against 'bad' or 'wrong' moves by other improvisers (which are actually just different to theirs). They sometimes announce out loud what will decidedly happen in the next scene in order to control the show.

Good Thinkers are ready to drop their heavy concepts at a moment's notice. They also let the show as a whole be determined by the group and not by them as an individual. They are great lateral thinkers and inspire originality.

The Caretaker

Caretakers love to help their scene partner. They see what's happening in a scene and do whatever is needed. They are just as happy playing strong characters as they are initiating a verbal 'follow-me' scene. They will initiate just as much as not.

Caretakers avoid freedom. On paper they are the perfect improviser, doing whatever is needed. And though you'll get a good solid show every time from a Caretaker, it won't be a life-changer. Caretakers avoid just fucking around. They want to know what is needed and how they should do it. They don't take enough risks or ever really surprise themselves.

Bad Caretakers do too much. They see a fun scene going on and they want to get in there, as a walk-on, as a scene-paint, as another character. Sometimes scenes need it of course, but bad Caretakers overdo it. It's not a lack of trust; they just want to play.

Good Caretakers are just as happy ending up as the lead as they are being one of the chorus line. They see what the show needs and they step in selflessly.

No one type is better than another.

146

The Maydays talked about whether it was a good idea to have a balance of these types cast in our shows, but were more excited by the idea that we could all be freed up to serve the show.

Stretch

In order to serve the show and your fellow players, you will often need to work against feeling comfortable and expand your range as an improviser. Have a stretch.

Putting us into these three types of Clown, Thinker and Caretaker is a nice, broad way of getting into personal work, but we are all more complex and subtle than that. You can think of it more as a bank of faders where each is labelled differently. There is a sliding scale between styles of physical and verbal work, big and small characters and the pace of play.

Try moving the faders around for your own work. Here are some areas you can try.

Initiating/responding

An initiation is the first thing that happens in a scene, the thing that starts it. It can be physical or verbal. The initiator is sometimes obvious to the audience and sometimes not. In a premise-driven show, that person will often step onto the stage first (even if it is indiscernible to the audience) and deliver a line or do a physical action delivering information to the other player(s). If you are doing a more organic show, you may be the first on stage but you'll find the content of the scene together with your partner.

Try initiating, finding things together and waiting for the other person to initiate. Can you find other notches on that scale?

Cartoony/realistic characters

Do you tend to play characters that are very close to yourself or do you always go for big wacky characters? Perhaps it's somewhere in between?

Try a scene where you play yourself, then turn up the wacky in every subsequent scene.

Physical/verbal

Do you do a lot of silent scenes with physical play or do you stand still and talk the whole time? Perhaps it's somewhere in between?

148

Play five scenes. In the first, make sure there is no silence between dialogue. In each subsequent scene, turn up the silence until the fifth scene has no dialogue at all. See how your physicality changes.

Quick fire/slow

Do you work quickly – probably with jokes and fast edits – or do you take time to find the subtext?

Play a few scenes where each one is edited quickly, then play some much longer ones. Does it change how you play?

Emotional/logical

Are your choices felt or thought out? Do you tend to have an emotional reaction to another move in a scene or a cerebral one?

Have someone tell a real-life monologue. Using this as your inspiration, try some scenes where you enter only when you have a comedy-sketch idea. Using a new monologue, try some scenes where you lead with an emotional choice based on the feeling you got from the monologue or an emotion that was mentioned in it.

Stretch exercise

Add more faders to this list and experiment with turning each up and down. In a group, try appointing a 'caller' to start each scene. Have the caller announce a percentage, then name one of the faders. "Eighty per cent character" will mean something pretty cartoony and wacky. "Five per cent physical" will mean using a lot of dialogue and little action.

The Introvert and the Extrovert

I ride the line between introvert and extrovert, though being with people depletes rather than recharges me as a person, so I am a little more on the introvert side. Improv is a great tool for both introverts and extroverts. After years of improv, I find it much easier to talk to new people in the real world!

The good thing is that improv bigs up the great parts about introverts and extroverts alike and lessens the jarring extremes. For one, we are not being competitive: we are not trying to be the funniest but are using our skills to make one another look good. Gags and upstaging are seen as rookie traits in improv. If they're done by experienced teams they're done knowingly whilst serving the show and taking care of one another. If the same guy is in every scene and upstaging in every show, there is a problem. That is extrovert at its worst. Equally, if an introvert isn't getting on stage, we are in trouble, because we are not supported. Ideally, we all meet in the middle.

There's an expectation that comedians should be funny offstage as well as on. I don't think it'll be news to you that some are and some aren't. Certainly there are many huge stars (like Rowan Atkinson) who are well known for being introverts. Who cares? If you're doing comedy so that strangers can be impressed by your job/hobby there's more self-care that needs to happen!

If performing makes you nervous, it is super-useful to turn your nerves into excitement. It really is much easier than you think. If you keep telling yourself that you're excited, you'll believe it. Yes, there are unpleasant nerves too, I feel them sometimes – especially when I'm doing script – but without that bit, you don't get the big high afterwards.

Don't worry if you're introverted or extroverted – comedy doesn't seem to fit with the mainstream. Like music, comedy is a taste that's different for everyone. The rhythm of reggae literally makes me cross and I can't tell you why I dislike Bob Dylan's voice. I like performing comedy where a small group loses their shit and everyone else looks around like: "What the fuck is funny about that?"

I would say a 'natural' improviser is less someone who's always telling jokes in public and more someone who is watching and listening; the one who is taking it all in. If you're constantly generating, how can you observe?

I feel pressure to be an extrovert as a teacher sometimes. There is a need for there to be high energy in an improv class. You don't want people to feel awkward; you want them to feel safe and excited. Doing things like playing music before we start and doing games that I love really help me with that. However, at no point am I pretending to be an extrovert: I use the exercises that make me feel comfortable, excited and challenged and I introduce them to the class. As a student, I find it hard when I have teachers that are too bubbly; their overexuberance can be tiring and sometimes feels fake. Grounded, clever teachers who clearly love what they do are my favourite. Chicago Improv Studio's Bill Arnett is one of my biggest influences and he quietly, apologetically takes a class with art-changing wisdom and it certainly doesn't drop the energy in the room; it focuses it. Bouncy teachers who are just naturally outgoing are also inspirational of course – like Jorin Garguilo – who must have seen all of this shit before but laughs at everything! Sincerity is the key; we don't have to pretend to be extroverts, or introverts for that matter. Honesty is always more compelling.

If you are introverted, it is really important to manage your energy before a show. If it takes you a while to warm up into performance mode, don't apologise for that; make sure people put in the time to get you into that headspace. Just like you would do for them.

If you are extroverted, your energy can make the show too frenetic. Make sure that you take the time to check in and connect with your fellow players. Play some focusing games and remember to breathe.

The Inner Critic

'The Inner Critic' is the voice inside of us that tells us we're unattractive, stupid, untalented and destined for failure. My Inner Critic loves to commentate on my work. Here is my critical monologue from points during writing this book:

> "Why are you writing this book? What's the point? You don't have enough experience to be writing about this stuff. You've never written a book before. People won't like you mentioning them. The teachers you quote are going to be pissed off. No one will buy it. You're too precious over the material to have anyone edit it objectively. You will make some glaring errors that you'll be embarrassed about for years. Who gives a shit about your opinion? Why not just write a bunch of exercises down instead of having big essays on improv self-help topics? Do you realise how niche this is? No one will be interested. You should get a real job: something more reliable than improv and acting..."

This monologue, of course, lives on during rehearsals too. Last week I took a workshop in London with a teacher from LA. My brain said:

> "None of these people know who you are and yet you've been teaching in Brighton and London for twelve years and globally for most of that time."

And the Inner Critic's monologue goes on in shows:

> "Okay, you've fucked this up already. You named him something and now you can't remember what it was. You've done one of your go-to characters. Friends in the audience will totally recognise that and think you're rubbish."

And so forth. It's exhausting and it doesn't matter what your level of experience is, it can haunt you at any time!

What if a friend talked to me like this? I wouldn't be friends with them. They would be a dick. So why put up with it from myself? When your Inner Critic becomes more loathing, you are doing something right. It shouts louder when you're successful or achieving something. So when I hear it taking over, I know I'm raising the bar for myself. If I'm finding this task difficult, that's good for me. If I suck; great, I can suck less next time with all the lessons I've learned. Sometimes my Inner Critic might have a point, but I need to unpick that and focus on the useful bits. If I'm worried that this show is awful, then I need to commit much harder and find things that make it fun. If I just bail on it, then my Inner Critic has won. Defeat the Inner Critic by taking action. Write the book, go for a jog, do the audition, meet the guy. If you don't take action, the outcome is definitely failure. If you do, you'll either learn, succeed or have a great story to tell.

Inner critic exercises

Write down some of the things your Inner Critic tells you over the next week. Look out for words like "never" and "always" and figure out if they are true. I bet they're not.

1. **What shit do you give yourself in rehearsal?**

For example: "I'm terrible at this exercise, I should be much better by now."

2. **What shit do you give yourself in class?**

For example: "These people must think I'm an asshole. I'm pretty sure they don't want to hang out at lunch."

3. What shit do you give yourself in a show?

For example: "I'm not in the right mood. This is going to be a terrible show."

4. What shit do you give yourself when you're being creative in any capacity?

For example: "No one will be interested in what I have to say."

Look for recurring worries. I know I always worry about 'character'. I don't think I'm good enough at it and yet, when I hit a good one, the show is so much easier and better than ever.

Decide what action you'll take to silence the Inner Critic

1.

For example: "The only way to get better at improv is to keep doing it. Also, it's fun!"

2.

For example: "Ask them if they want to have lunch (they do)."

154

> **3.**

For example: "What's my favourite warm-up? That'll put me in a better mood and I'll have a more fun show."

> **4.**

For example: "Who cares? Active reflection on my work will help in the long term. Keep writing, keep improvising, be creative."

It is also possible to externalise your Inner Critic and project it onto your team-mates or circumstances outside of the show. I know I've sometimes been critical to fellow players because I didn't like the work I did in a show.

Treat yourself well, like a good friend would. If you're feeling bad or like you can't do something, reassure yourself; treat yourself. Don't ruminate on things that didn't work; look forward to getting better. A two-minute distraction can be enough to stop me ruminating.

Fear

Fear is one of the best and worst things about improvisation. Muggles think improvisers are hardcore. There are regularly audience members who say: "I couldn't do that", "I'd be too scared", "You're so brave", and so forth. There is a classic nightmare where you end up on stage not knowing your lines. The thing is, we are all improvising all the time. Your conversations in real life are not scripted. What's easier: learning a bunch of lines that you could get wrong or just talking and acting like a person does? The scary part is, of course, getting up in front of an audience and fulfilling the promise of entertainment. The best way to achieve that is by managing our fear of it.

My fear of spiders totally ruined a holiday in Turkey when we rented an apartment that turned out to be full of big ones. I didn't lie on the pool loungers because I'd seen spiders there and my husband had to sweep the room for them before I went to bed. I am going to Thailand next week, so I went to a class to cure me of my arachnophobia. It worked. A lifetime phobia cured in an afternoon. If you are scared of improvising (or anything else), use it, transform it, or get over it.

If you don't trust, you fear – fear creates self-preservation. If you're only looking after yourself, you're not taking care of your scene partner.

Fear for me seems to change over the course of improvisation and it's different for different people. I was not scared at the beginning. In fact, improv gave me freedom in my drama class that I didn't have in the playground. Doing things 'wrong' was encouraged. It was salve to the horrific wound of correctness that my world had given me up to that point. In French lessons, I was told to stop checking everything in the textbook or dictionary before I spoke, but I didn't want to get it wrong and I didn't trust myself to be perfect. In improv, I don't have time to double-check and make things perfect. I have to be in the moment.

I definitely had the arrogance of youth when I started going to a local improv drop-in class in Brighton. Now sometimes in a room full of improvisers I catch myself thinking: "I'm supposed to be good." I sometimes feel like I have to prove all of the guidelines that I've been teaching. Project2 did a show a few nights ago where we were all characters trapped in a cursed lamp. I was the newcomer in the scene and was, asking a lot of questions about the lamp and how it worked. The scene was going fine, but I was running the rules "Don't ask questions" and "Don't be new here" in my head. Actually, it was a genre show where it was perfectly in keeping with a Disney narrative to play a fish out of water who gets to know how their world works. Still, I was outside of the scene looking down on myself as a director. The scene worked, but I was running the programme not having fun.

There are passive and aggressive responses to fear on stage. Some people shut down and shut up, and others attack and overcompensate.

Symptoms of Fear

Pimping your scene partner

"Do that stupid dance you do", "What was that rhyming poem you were quoting to me earlier?" Pimping isn't the loveliest word and hopefully improv will adopt something else, but it's still current parlance. It's not always a bad choice to 'pimp'. In a group with people you know and trust, it can be a lot of fun.

> "Between improvisers who trust each other there's no difference between a pimp and a gift. You know they won't give you stuff that makes you look bad."
> Craig Cackowski

A good way of figuring out if it's bad or good is to think: "Would I like this to happen to me?" If not, probably don't do it. Also, are you doing it because you're scared and you're just throwing the focus at the other player while you catch your breath? The best cure for this is to pimp yourself instead. Announce that you will read out your own rhyming poem or do a silly dance. That way, the other player(s) can choose to join in or take over with their beautiful support. You will get the same joyous audience reaction to your pimping, but you will be taking on the responsibility rather than panicking and making someone else take care of the show.

Watching the show go by

If you are frozen at the side of the stage and your feet won't move to edit or be in a scene it can be pretty tough. Keep trying to get in there. My tactic is just to get into the first or second scene. That way, I get out of my head early and I'm already in the show. If I never make the stage again (I will), then at least I did one scene. The longer you wait, the more stress there is about 'fucking up'. You'll worry about contradicting something that's been said, about editing at the 'wrong' time and so forth. The main thing – even if you don't manage to get yourself on stage – is to keep paying attention. Someone might call you on or physically pull you on stage and you're going to need to know what's happening so that you can play! Of course, you'll have a much worse time not going on stage than you would even going on and fucking it all up. That's what we're all there to do: justify each other's fuck-ups and make one another look good.

Forgetting to listen (especially to names)

You named the other player but the name has gone straight out of your head! Or they named you and you can't remember that. *Or* there were two names already and you can't remember either and maybe worst of all (and most frequent) you can't remember if anyone has been named, so you don't give anyone a name in case it's wrong. Stress sometimes means that we focus inwards and stop listening as carefully as we should to ourselves or our scene partner.

Try and repeat any name at least three times out loud in the scene. Overuse it. It's amazing just how many times you can use a name without it being super-weird. Don't use the same fall-back name every time; be creative and it will be a gift to your fellow improviser.

Selling your scene partner out

You call out a bad accent, point out a wrong name or generally throw your scene partner under the bus for a one-off laugh that will probably cut the scene short. I'm not suggesting you ignore these things; errors are the fuel of improv, but the way to treat them is to justify them. If someone has been given two names is it because they are leading a double life or they have a double-barrelled name? If someone has a crazy accent, do you even need to call it out? Perhaps it's fine as it is, or you can praise them for being well-travelled and exotic or invent the name of a new country you've always wanted to visit.

Doing every idea you have

You don't need to be on stage one hundred per cent of the time (unless you're doing a form where that is a thing, like a Cat's Cradle, a solo show or a duo where that's your artistic decision). If you're in a show with six people, you should imagine that a sixth of the show is yours; much more or much less than that means that you're over- or undercompensating. After throwing my way into the first or second scene, I'll have

159

beaten my demons and then be in the right headspace to watch actively for when I can serve the show as a writer and actor.

I watched a show at the Edinburgh Fringe where one actor in a six-person show was in every scene (where scenes were mostly two people). She was mouthing words when her scene partner was speaking and impatiently waiting for her turn. She also did a lot of walk-ons in other scenes, which did not add, but let the air out of them. The one scene where she was offstage, she literally threw objects onto the stage that the actors had to bat away and justify.

The confusing thing for an improviser is that you will get positive reinforcement for these moves from the audience. There is a rhythm to interruption that creates laughter, so the moves were often funny ones, but the cost of them was very high. The scenes themselves were broken and we didn't get to experience the full emotional and comedy potential. The physical interruptions were just plain rude. It's fun to play in this way – to do every comedy idea that comes into your head – but ultimately it's selfish. You will win but the show will lose. The show's other improvisers did a great job of pushing back and performing brilliantly. If this improviser only did half of her ideas, she would have been an asset to the show rather than a stick in the wheel.

Largely this is about experience and stage time. After a certain number of shows, you are less desperate to prove yourself and your ego may settle and be content with making excellent work, rather than being a player that people might remember. Even if the audience likes you, the ensemble may not. Doing too much is another version of selling your scene partner out.

Overtalking

This is one I'm guilty of. When I'm not totally relaxed or when I'm with a one-night team, I might overcompensate by saying too much. I sometimes talk over my scene partner, or I don't leave enough space for them to get in. At my best I will play slow and with great subtext, emotion and connection, but overtalking is my 'fear' choice. It's a way of being in control. When you worry that your scene partner might not 'have this', you look after them too much. But the important thing about improv is that we must trust our scene partner even if they haven't done a day of improv training in their lives.

My friend Neil Curran does a show called *Neil +1* where he gets an audience member who has never done improv before, interviews them and then performs an hour of two-person improv with them. Neil is so generous a scene partner that he sees everything as the most perfect offer. With no training, his cohort will often break the reality, criticise, question or even want to leave! Neil is the ultimate professional, however, and he will justify and 'yes-and' everything he gets. Neil is never the hero of this show: it's always the guest that walks away like royalty. He has the perfect balance of leading and following where he trusts this completely green player to be a genius, artist and poet, as we all aspire to be.

Making someone else the expert

Saying "It's my first day" or any other version of "I don't know" at the top of a scene is a 'fear' choice. Asking someone else to be the teacher, the surgeon, the gym instructor or the top scientist is another pimp. You're asking the other player to come up with all of the specifics and to coach you through the scene. Play as if you know what you're doing. You don't have to get it 'right'. If you're the world's top surgeon, you don't have to use the correct terms: make some up; use ones that sound like they'd be in a hospital drama. Whatever you say in this world becomes true of this world. The audience knows you are improvising, they don't expect you truly to be an expert, only to act like one.

Asking questions

In and of itself, asking questions is not a bad thing, because we do that in our daily conversations to be polite and interested humans and it sounds realistic on stage. However, asking questions because you don't want to make decisions puts pressure on the other player to justify the scene: "Where are we?", "Who are you?", "What's that in your hand?" These are all defences that make your scene partner have to work hard. If you have a question in your head, go ahead and answer it: "Here we are at the garden centre", "Mum...", "I see you're taking the cat to the vet, finally."

Berating yourself

Even if you do a great show and make lots of excellent choices, fear can manifest after a show as self-doubt. You can worry that you messed it up for the other performers; that you were just terrible and you should stop doing improv. Listen to the opinions of other people, receive and enjoy compliments (don't dodge them or explain why they're wrong) and decide from whom it is useful to take criticism. If you're really not enjoying improv or it's too scary, take time off. It's supposed to be fun! Sometimes we overload ourselves with classes and coaching and we have too many things to implement before we're happy with our work. Do work on things but don't work on everything all the time. Let one good practice at a time become muscle memory until your work becomes more instinctual. If you're still not having fun and making a lot of fear choices, ask yourself:

> "Are you in the right team?"
> "Are you being supported?"
> "What brought you into improv?"
> "What were your favourite things about it?"

Underselling your ideas

As well as selling out your fellow improvisers, you can really give yourself a bad time. Pointing out when you did something that didn't work within the scene or delivering a line without commitment makes everything harder. In improv, every idea is good, but that's because every idea is used as if it were the best. Undercommitting is a way of protecting yourself. If the audience doesn't laugh or react in the way you want, you defend yourself by pretending you didn't want or need that reaction. "Yeah, I know it was a shit idea, so what?"

Good job! You've made it to the end of Week Six.

Let's go through our weekly practice checklist.

Read

Did you read the chapter? Of course you did!

Improvise

Clowns, Thinkers and Caretakers Exercises

- Decide for yourself or with your group if you primarily fit into one of these three types.
- Write out the missions below on different coloured cards or Post-It notes. Each is based on a behaviour that type avoids doing.
- Have a pile for each type to draw from and do a run of scenes using these secret suggestions.
- Please go ahead and add your own; the cards should be something that type does not normally do.
- Now use these as the inspiration for a set of scenes, having people draw a different one from their category every time they go on stage.

Cards for Clowns

Endow your scene partner (tell them who they are or something about them).

Find or create game in the scene.

Be highly specific about everything you mention.

Drive the scene.

Build the platform (who, what, where) in one line.

Do a scene backwards.

Do a strong verbal edit.

Initiate.

Start with a one-line 'follow-me'.

Play yourself.

Pimp your scene partner.

You are the best at everything.

React honestly as *you* would.

Cards for Thinkers

Choose a silly voice.

Match your scene partner's energy.

Have an expressive character noise (like a sigh or a laugh).

Enter with a strange physicality.

Play someone you know.

Play physically close to your scene partner.

Do this scene like there's jelly in your pants.

Only use words your scene partner has used.

Switch between angry and wistful.

Start the scene by saying "Fuck, fuck, fuck!"

Play an animal.

Do an accent *loudly*.

Do some slapstick.

Cards for Caretakers

Fuck around.

Strike an unusual pose.

Touch the other improviser as much as possible.

Be an object or animal that can't speak.

Make your scene partner laugh.

Enter and exit as much as possible.

Say a line that has no relevance to anything.

[This card is just a picture of a tree.]

Scene-paint something that does not tie in with the scene.

Break the rules.

Be selfish.

Dance.

Do a scene with noises instead of words.

Talk about the work afterwards

> Did your work change?
>
> Was it harder/easier?
>
> Did you find a difference in your team?
>
> What will you change about the way you improvise?
>
> Did any of the suggestions scare you and, if so, why?

You can also swap around and play other types or try several to discover the things you avoid doing!

I know that when I experimented with this, I was relieved not to be leading scenes as much and I found new trust in my team. It turns out I'd rather follow and take endowments, but I just don't give people time to do that. I don't take as many big risks as I could – probably for the same reason: trust – but now I will.

The Maydays learned that when Clowns initiate a game, when Thinkers do a silly voice, and when Caretakers fuck around, magic happens.

INTROVERT AND EXTROVERT EXERCISES

Pre-show exercises for introverts

- Have people suggest five different character monologues for you to play in quick succession.
- Try and touch your partner's knees before they touch yours!
- Perform mini-scenes using your fingers as the players.

Pre-show exercises for extroverts

- Count from one to twenty as a group with only one person talking at a time. If more than one person speaks at one time, start again.
- Tell a story one word at a time with a different person saying each word.
- Have each person describe the imagined character of the person to their right. "This is the Great Magician of Monmouth; he is always at the head of the dinner table, he loves to read long books and design magic tricks involving birds."

Even more exercises

- Pimp yourself to do something difficult or silly in a scene.
- In your rehearsal this week, every time someone is named for the first time, have everyone in the room shout that name back. It will really help you to notice and remember names. Keep using the names throughout the scene.
- Give everyone in your group five pieces of paper (or tokens or sweets). Do a set where everyone has to spend a piece of paper (or eat a sweet) every time they come on stage. That includes sweep edits, voices offstage or anything where you are adding. Once you have spent your papers, you cannot add to the show. Chat afterwards about how this felt.
- Do a scene where one improviser has permission to 'break improv'. Allow them to do the worst improv they possibly can while you justify their actions and help the scene to work. Switch.

Watch

Did you manage to see a show?

What was it?

Reflect

Write down your notes or thoughts on what you read, saw or did this week.

Week Seven:
Form and Style

There are guidelines for improvisation but no one set of rules that make your choices clear in every show. Choosing the form of your show and the style within that show can help you to make those choices on stage and enable your team to be cohesive in their art. This week we look at style and form, breaking established forms, the specifics of the Living Room, and the challenges of two-person improv.

Form

As with films, novels, plays and comics, there is no one structure or definitive way to structure an improv show. There are many, many forms. The Harold is our most famous longform structure, and schools often teach the Harold as your first structured improv show. It teaches you how and when to edit, how to bring characters back, how to generate ideas as a team and how to explore theme. If a teacher tells you that there is one way to do a Harold, then what they are really saying is: "This is how I learned and how my school teaches a Harold." Originally Del Close's Harold form came out of having improvisers play and seeing what worked, not starting with a structure that came out of his head. I'd recommend learning the Harold and using it as training wheels until the techniques above become second nature.

There are lots of other classic American forms like the Deconstruction, the Pretty Flower, the Bat, the Armando, the Slacker, etc., or you can design your own. There are lots of books and online resources giving you all of these structures in detail, so I'm going to look at form more generally.

Each part of a form has a different function for a show.

Audience suggestion

An audience suggestion or call-out is the classic way of proving that you're making the show up as you go along. They make the audience feel like they're part of the show and they inspire the team to create something totally new.

If you don't want to take an audience suggestion, find something that inspires the team in a different way. I have seen a few groups use: the music from someone's phone, tweets, Wikipedia articles, the blurb from the back of a book, a play or festival brochure and so forth. Rachel and I take a look at each other when the lights come up (inspired by TJ and Dave) and use the physical and emotional information we get to start the show.

Opening

The opening is the part of the show where the audience suggestion is explored. It often uses all of the improvisers so that everyone is able to throw out theme ideas, warm up with the audience and get more in tune with one another. The opening can be organic or heavily structured like a kind of theatrical shortform game. This is the well that the rest of the show drinks from.

Scenes

Scenes are the mainstay of our art form. They are different to openings and game beats. They can often stand alone but are more powerful within a form. Some forms have a very specific number of scenes and guidelines about which scenes revisit particular characters, themes or locations.

Game beats

Game beats are re-energisers and an exploration of a new angle on a theme, or a palate cleanser or reset button for the show. Whatever your opening was, other game beats will likely be similar and happen a few times throughout the show. For example, you might have three organic group beats to break up the scenes and give you new inspiration, or a brand-new monologue when the first one feels like it has been thoroughly explored.

A good description of a form as a whole is that it starts with a thesis (the opening), explores the thesis (with scenes and game beats) then concludes with whether or not the thesis was correct (the final scenes).

Genre forms

I'm talking about shows like *Improvised Shakespeare, Austentatious: The Improvised Jane Austen Novel, Murder She Didn't Write, Improvised Star Trek* and so on. The form of a genre show will likely mirror the structure of the source material. If you wanted to do improvised *Memento*, you would be performing a series of scenes that each took place before the last. If you were performing a horror genre, your form might start with a lot of scenes introducing the characters, then a bunch more scenes having them killed off, with the ending being a parallel of Carrie's hand coming out of the grave.

Narrative

A narrative show may also be a genre piece. It means that you will be doing something along the lines of the Hero's Journey with a protagonist and a beginning, middle and end to the story.

When I coach narrative, the number-one problem is that people add too much information. When you get halfway into the show, stop adding! New characters, facts and story expectations can leave you with too much and the end of the show will be a lot of people quickly trying to tie up loose ends. Establish the world at the beginning and find out who has the biggest 'want'. They will probably get what they want halfway through, then realise that it didn't solve their real problem. They'll find their way back to the start having changed.

Styles of Play

There is no one way to improvise but it is very helpful to define how you are going to play. When I coach, I check in with the group to find out what they are going for and that helps me steer them in the scenes. There is so much contradictory advice in improv, but most of it is context-specific. If you want to do gags in a show as opposed to lifelike character exploration, then you need to use different techniques. If the actors in your company are all playing different styles, it might stop the show from being as solid as you would like.

> "Warm up appropriate to the show you are doing."
> Bill Arnett

Even the Harold can be performed in many different styles. It can be done focusing on premise scenes or using slow-burn truthful character work. You can also blend various approaches, as long as your team is in tune enough to know which approach a particular scene needs.

Premise

I find it helpful to think of premise shows as improvised sketch. The first person on stage is normally telling their partner the idea they have for a sketch in a line of dialogue and the two (or more) of them then play out the game. Premise shows often use source material like a monologue, newspaper clippings or confessions. Shows like *Whirled News Tonight* in Chicago play this way, as do The Maydays in *Confessions* and *Tonight's Top Story*. UCB shows are often game and premise-driven.

Using your source material, find something that stands out to you: a turn of phrase, an emotion, a strange situation. Then discern what's funny about that thing. Look at how you can change the specifics to make it a new sketch. Get that idea across to your fellow player(s) with an initiation. That initiation should give them the who, what and where of the scene and the angle you want to play.

Game can be used for good or evil

I was coaching a two-person show last night. One of the lines (referring to sex) was "That sounds like a criticism of my technique." It was a lovely line to build a game off. Now the first player can passive aggressively criticise how the other character does everything. "If you shake the pan, the eggs will stop sticking" and so forth. The improvisers were surprised that they could use game in this way and not just for high-concept moves. Doing something as subtle as a character game along with everything else can be really satisfying and helps give you a strong point of view. Game is often perceived as a hard and fast way of playing: a big, immediate escalation of a comedic situation. Find the tiny, subtle ways of using it as a conversational game. Both characters can have one as well as the scene. Even the environment can have a game at the same time. Look out for the first unusual thing or 'mistake' and recycle that in new and interesting ways, or create something at odds with the scene yourself. You don't have to wait for game to arrive; you can extricate it from any line or physical offer.

Slow burn

This is the home of TJ and Dave who imagine that they are just stepping into an hour or so of their characters' lives. The show is often in real time (or close) and the characters feel like real people. If you're interested in playing this way, their book *Improvisation at the Speed of Life* is excellent.

This style is how Rachel and I play. We start the show 'amused and interested', playing characters that are close to ourselves. We focus largely on natural silences and subtext. There are no high dramas in the show (we might have one moment of revelation). We draw from our real lives to find the characters in the show. We have a lot of conversations about everyday things which give us an idea of how these people think and who they are. Every word is important and how things are said gives us a wealth of information.

Genre

Genre shows parody or emulate the source material and that is your style. You can either use the known characters or a new batch of similar characters that exist in the same world. Know your genre, don't just go for the well-known traits, do the research. Film noir is not just people smoking cigarettes, it often explored the emerging psychology at the time, moral ambiguity and post-war cynicism. Watch, read and learn as much as you can before you break the show down and build it back up. I mentioned my *Quantum Leap* show earlier, which slightly broke improv in order to successfully emulate the TV show. Look at style of speech, the type of characters and the tropes from your source material. If it feels like that genre, that will be the most important thing, even if your structure is a little different or less narrative.

Coens' Gloves (or Why I'm Bored of Chekhov's Gun)

You've probably heard of the theatre term 'Chekhov's Gun', it comes up in narrative improv as much as Schrödinger's Cat comes up in science fiction.

> "If you say in the first chapter that there is a rifle hanging on the wall, in the second or third it absolutely must go off. If it's not going to be fired, it shouldn't be hanging there."
> Anton Chekhov

Let me open with the fact that I do both narrative and freeform improv shows, so if this sounds negative, it's not meant that way. I absolutely thrill while I jot my *Oh Boy! The Quantum Leap Show* structure on the blackboard and our Tim Burton-style musical is as Hero's Journey as they come; but let's talk about the opposite of Chekhov's Gun and how exciting and freeing it can be. I'm going to call it Coens' Gloves.

I love the TV show *Fargo* and was so happy to hear this story when it was told in one of the episodes:

> "There's a fella once, running for a train — and he's carrying a pair of gloves, this man. He drops a glove on the platform, but he doesn't notice. And then later on, inside the train, he's sitting by the window and he realises that he's just got this one glove left. But the train's already started pulling out of the station, right? So what does he do? He opens the window. And he drops the other glove onto the platform. That way, whoever finds the first glove can just have the pair."

I loved this parable in the show. Lots of people debated what it meant and why the character told the story. The writer – actually Noah Hawley and not the Coen brothers – talked about how the Coens use various stories and moments in their films that pertain to nothing. Life is full of irrelevances, of strange and incongruent moments. The writer fought for this story staying in his script and won, despite the fact that it was not part of the plot (or even character development, necessarily). Hawley was emulating the style of the Coen brothers and therefore emulating the randomness of human existence.

> "Once you take away that Joseph Campbell Journey bullshit... then you're doing something that people can't predict as well... but it has to be satisfying."
> Noah Hawley

Not everything you do in improv has to serve the story. That doesn't mean you can drop information or pay less attention, it means that you can choose what is important to the story as well as what is important to the feel, style or genre of the show. Let's not follow the road well travelled. I would rather watch (or play in) a show where I'm surprised and delighted at what is happening than honour a plot that is predictable and clichéd. One of the most fun things about improv is how it differs from writing; that we discover something more organic than perfectly driven narrative and something that can only be produced by the group mind in this moment. Freeform improv is a discipline. It doesn't mean going straight to wacky land or adding too much information. It's just as hard or easy as telling a neat story and when you're good at that neat story, you can decide to get off the path.

It's *Fargo*'s emulation of truth that I love the most about improv and if truth means leaving Chekhov's Gun on the wall for the whole show, I'm down with it. Perhaps that unfired gun will hang there as a metaphor for the emotional impotence of one of our characters, portend a darker future or prompt the audience to think about their own guns (their potential, their rage, their secrets). One thing that narrative and freeform agree on, however, is that whatever that gun is there for, it's important.

What is Your Solo Show?

Choosing what show to do is often the hardest part. You're willing, you're excited, but without other players with whom to reach a shared vision, your choices can seem infinite. What do you like to do? What is your favourite style or level of characterisation? Is there something you are really passionate about that exists outside of improv?

Solo show exercises (inspired by Jill Bernard)

Answer these questions to find out what excites you!

- Do you have a hobby that isn't improvisation (hula-hooping, sewing, reading, ancient history, dance, languages)?
- Is there a film director you really like?
- What was the last great piece of theatre you saw?
- What makes you laugh? (In life and in entertainment.)
- Which TV shows are you currently enjoying?
- Which person or people inspire you? It could be someone famous or someone close to you. My student Constantine Pavlou used his family to inspire his solo show.
- Do you like interacting with an audience?
- Will you use props?

I'll give you more on creating a format later, but these are your first steps towards inspiration. Also, you aren't stuck inside an idea or format. If you do it for a few shows or rehearsals and you're not having fun, change it. But really try it before you do; good things take work. And finally, go easy on yourself. You are likely your worst critic, so make sure you take the time to be kind to yourself.

Write down anything you enjoyed, made you laugh or felt like an interesting choice at the end of your rehearsal (or show). Lines of dialogue, character ideas, settings, objects and concepts can all be fuel later.

Twoprov

The great thing about two-person improvisation is that you get to play a lot more than you would in an ensemble show. Sure, you might be doing a form where everyone's on the whole time, but you are still making a smaller percentage of the decisions. You will get to know yourself more as an improviser and it will feel both harder and easier than ensemble shows. Harder because you're probably on the whole time and easier because you don't have a lot of time to think.

I spent over eleven years playing with Rachel and five years doing two-person shows with Chris Mead and Jonathan Monkhouse in Project2. Then there are all the occasional shows I have played like *Messing With a Friend* and with Lloydie James Lloyd, Rhiannon Vivian, Maria Peters and many others. The point is, every single one of those combinations breeds a completely different show. When I'm playing with Jon, we tend to produce a slower, creepier science-fiction horror. With Susan I mirror, or play opposite and create a lot of huge fucked-up characters and try to keep emotional reactions as big as the horrifying world we build. Playing with Rhiannon begets a slow real-world scene that builds to something surreal or bizarrely heightened, etc. I'm sure that when these improvisers are paired with other people, that crossover creates another dynamic again.

The best way to discover what kind of show you produce with another improviser is just to do one. Even if it's a 'terrible' show, you'll find out how and when you wanted to edit, what excited you about the other person, what your pacing is and such. Ideally afterwards, but also before, you can draw a Venn diagram to see what you both love to do. If you're both into broad brushstroke characters and silly situations and you fall into a Harold without thinking about it (me and Maria Peters) then that's what to work on. Flesh out those characters a little, heighten those silly situations and dig into or out of the format.

Twoprov warm-up exercises

Physical

Facing one another, have one of you hold your palm out face down. The other improviser puts their palm upwards, touching it. The person with their hand on top moves the other player around the space. The follower (hand beneath) pushes gently upwards, maintaining contact the whole time and being fluidly led. Swap around to try a different leader and follower. Now repeat the exercise but with the follower's eyes closed. It's a great game for moving fluidly, connecting and trusting your partner. It's pretty meditative too.

Mental

"I NEED..."

(I learned this from Bill Arnett.) Give a list of three things to the other player.

"I need a pencil, a rubber and a sheet of paper."

Then they take the last thing on the list and make a new list starting with that.

"I need a sheet of paper, some stickers and some glitter."

"I need some glitter, a nightclub and a thong."

And so forth. You can play this slowly with well-thought-out lists or fast where the lists just fall out however they do. It depends what kind of show you do as to which would be the most useful.

Character

CHARACTER TRADE

Facing each other, one will create an abstract sound and motion. The other improviser waits for this to become solidified, then copies it as exactly as they can. When it's mirrored closely, the first improviser drops their sound and action and the copier adds a monologue to it. Go for the most obvious thing you can; if it sounds like a barking army general, be that. What voice does this sound morph into? Is it high-pitched or low, staccato or loose and arrhythmic? What does the body do? Is this action something the character uses to punctuate their words, is it a nervous tic? Is it just a feature of how they stand? The monologue will be short, perhaps thirty seconds or so.

Swap roles so that the monologist now creates a new sound and motion for the other to follow. You can speed these up and trade them back and forth to create lots of new and interesting characters. Get in tune with one another and be physical. Rachel and I found that this helped our characters on stage be more varied. It also helped us trade characters on stage when we were doing scenes with more than two in them.

There's a twist to this game where you can add a third stage. When the character monologue has come out, the originator of the abstract sound and motion can take it back. This time, it is their job to add another layer to the character. If the character seems fairly obvious and somewhat 2D, give them something else. If it's a laddy character who talks about football to his mates and seems a bit of a cliché, have him talk about ballet for a bit. He loves it. He is really excited about the new production of *Coppélia* and amazed by the art itself, as well as the physical condition and commitment of the performers.

Setting the scene

Commentate on the other performer as they perform a physical task. Literally point out everything they are doing. You are not adding to this scene or guessing what they are doing, just say what you see. If you are not sure what they are doing, say that. Project2 learned this from our current coach, Tim Sniffen, and found it incredibly useful for paying attention to the object work and scene-setting the other performers are doing.

Emotion and subtext

Rachel and I use a Meisner exercise that we have likely perverted, but which we find very useful. Sit opposite one another on chairs with your knees touching. Make eye contact and take turns saying the phrase: "I'm watching you watching me." Keep eye contact the whole time. It will start by feeling a little bit weird and exposing. I know I'll be worried about what I look like at the start. Am I doing an odd expression, do I have snot coming out of my nose? I bet she notices that spot, etc. Then that will pass and you'll just get into the repetition. When you're absorbed with the exercise, go ahead and point out small things that you notice. You don't need to look for them, just mention them when they come up. "You raised your eyebrow", to which Rachel will respond: "I raised my eyebrow." This goes back and forth for a bit, then we return to:

"I'm watching you watching me." It feels very much like a wanky theatre exercise and that's because it is. However, the level of attention it affords you for the micro-cues of that other player is brilliant and it's definitely worth your time. After more than a decade this is still one of our top three warm-ups.

Have a chat

What? Yes, catch up. How was your day? What's going on with you? How are you feeling? Having a good idea of what your fellow improviser is feeling and going through will help you have a great show. Often the things we talk about before our shows show up on stage in tiny ways. Perhaps we talked about a friend's boyfriend and a version of them arrives as a character, perhaps we bemoaned something in the news and that might be mapped into a scene. It's not cheating or pre-planned, it's sharing a state of mind that may or may not influence your work.

Try doing two-person shows with a few different people and see how quickly you learn. When Susan Messing got too busy to do the many shows she was doing in Chicago, she asked herself – if she could just do one show – what would it be? The answer was a two-person show with a different guest every week and that is the now legendary *Messing With a Friend*.

The Living Room Format

I learned the Living Room as part of an iO class in 2013 taught by Charna Halpern. Afterwards Tony Harris and I played our version *At Home with Katy and Tony* at the Hoopla Comedy Club in London Bridge for a few years. The Maydays also perform it at the biannual improv retreat in Dorset. As with any format, things morph and change via different groups and teachers and this is the version I have ended up with.

I'm currently coaching this longform format for Classic Andy and All Made Up, as well as teaching it as part of my Hoopla advanced class. It's a nice simple one and fun to play. We'll look at this one in detail because it will help you design or finesse your own show in the next section.

History

Charna tells me that the form comes from longform group The Family. They would chat in Charna's living room and because they are improvisers, they would jump up and do scenes during their conversations. Charna loved watching them, so she took her living-room furniture to iO and asked The Family to improvise on stage exactly like they did in her home, beer-drinking included.

Structure

The format itself is very simple. There is a sofa on one side of the stage and an open playing space on the other with a couple of chairs. The form starts with an audience suggestion, the players chat, the players do one scene, the players chat, they do one scene, alternating scenes and chats until the time runs out.

Timing

The show can run from fifteen minutes up to an hour. If you do an hour, you should really make sure the pace changes, the stories evolve and characters come back. We've also played it where we do the show in two or three chapters where we switch up some of our guests for each one.

Number of players

In class, we used five or six players. On stage we sometimes had more. It's also possible to play the form with more people by allocating the chats to half the players and the scenes to the other half, perhaps with a switch in between. It's more fun if you all get to do everything, though.

The suggestion

This is what you get from the audience to begin your show. Tony and I would ask: "What's the weirdest house-warming present you ever received?", "Is there an object in your house you'd like to get rid of, but you can't?" or similar. We'd use the suggestion to inspire our conversation. You can ask for anything, though I wouldn't get an audience member's story, because you're about to do a bunch of chatting.

Chats

It's important that everything you talk about on the sofa is *true* and that you make that clear to the audience beforehand. It's generally more interesting if it's about you personally, rather than you telling a story third-hand. Be careful of falling into pop-culture conversations. It's more interesting to hear about your life and your opinions than it is to discuss what just happened in *Game of Thrones*. None of the chat part of the show has to be funny. The scenes generate the comedy. In fact, if you use up the funny on the sofa, it's sometimes harder to get ideas to bring into scenes. Rather than grilling other people on their stories, try and bring in your experiences. After the first beat, chats can be inspired by the call-out, by previous topics, or the scenes that have gone before.

Scenes

The scenes are 'follow-me'/premise-style, which means that improvisers will start a scene when they have an idea based on the conversation that is happening. You can do this any way you like, but here are some ways in:

MAPPING

Putting one situation on top of another; i.e. a familiar cop scenario – "You're just too much of a maverick, Kelly, I'm gonna need your badge and your gun" – mapped onto a flatmate disagreement might be: "You're just too much of a maverick, Dave, I'm gonna need your fridge space and my towel back."

GAME

A premise where the moves are laid out (or found) up top; i.e. you get angrier every time I mention ex-boyfriends. In this form, the game is likely to be laid out in the first line or two rather than found.

CHARACTER

Embody a character that was described and put them into the worst/best situation to bring out their characteristics.

EMOTION

Take the overwhelming emotion of the subject and put this into the worst/best scenario for it to be explored.

POINT OF VIEW

Use a strong point of view from the chat and set it in the worst/best scenario.

QUOTATIONS

If you particularly like a line that was said, quote it directly as the initiation of your scene or play in a world where it is super-important.

QUESTIONS

If you question something that was brought up within the chat – i.e. an incorrect fact or something you just don't understand or relate to – play it out.

EDITS

Edits are the moments when we move from a chat to a scene or vice versa.
- If you're on the sofa, edit by talking.
- If you're on the stage, edit by moving back to the sofa.

Tag-outs are where you replace one or more characters in the scene, therefore keeping one character from the previous scene. The idea is to add more information pertinent to what was just said or discovered and to cut back to the original scenario. To tag, tap the person(s) on the shoulder that you want to replace.

> • Tag runs are multiple version tag-outs where one character is kept in for three or more short scenes illustrating one point.

The timing of edits is different to other shows; you are not waiting for a *good* edit point from the sofa, like a laugh, the end of a story or an insight, you are merely waiting for an idea. As soon as you have one, edit. No matter how rude it may seem to do it then! We can always revisit the story and there's a lot of comedy to be had in following the inspiration. It's also much funnier to have a sofa than chairs because it's pretty awkward skipping onto the stage from a comfortable lounger. High-energy edits in this show are particularly important, as there is a lot of sitting and talking.

Other tips

- We discovered that sitting in a different seat on the sofa every time you returned was a nice way of changing up the energy.
- Drink beer; it makes the show feel different to a regular longform and makes you a little sillier and more confessional! The visual of people drinking on a sofa also helps transport the audience to a living-room atmosphere. That's optional of course!
- Dress the set with props that are living-room appropriate. Add a lamp, a picture and cushions.
- Remember that the audience is there! It's sometimes quite hypnotic talking to the other people, so talk out and remember to project your voice.
- Share as much or as little as you feel comfortable revealing in the show.
- Don't ask for specific stories from your friends on the sofa, they may have decided not to share for a reason!

Warm-ups for this style

EIGHT THINGS ABOUT ME

One person stands in the middle of the circle and says eight things that are true about them. Each is counted off by the team.

> "I used to have two pet rats."
> "One thing!"
> "I bleach my hair."
> "Two things!"

THAT MAKES ME THINK OF...

Stand in a circle. One person offers a word and someone says: "That makes me think of..." before launching into a true monologue or opinion. Immediately someone else in the circle has an idea based on a word in the monologue, they take over: "You said bread which makes me think of..." and so on. Make sure everyone gets in there.

TAG-OUT SCENES IN A CIRCLE (keeping one of the characters each time).

ANECDOTES

Three of you describe (to camera, mockumentary-style) a shared experience as suggested by your team, e.g. the time you made your first flan.

Your Format

Now let's make a cheat sheet for *your* show. It'll help you work out what you want it to look and feel like, give you an idea of how to warm up and how to see what was hard or easy after each performance. It'll also help you bring new members into the show and it can be updated as you go along making new discoveries.

History

Did you make this up and/or where did it come from? What inspired it and is there source material you can go back to to see what works? With genre shows, there will be loads to watch or read, so get to it. When we did *Oh Boy: The Quantum Leap Show*, we not only had to know all of the existing episodes but have a good idea of American and British history from the 1950s onwards. We all took a decade to start with and made simple sheets of famous songs, leaders and events from that time. By the end of the run we had swapped over the decades enough to be familiar with a lot of the info we needed.

Write down your history here.

Structure

Is this a narrative show? Perhaps you need to study the story structure. Can you look at the source material and work out what a general structure might be for each episode or novel? Or is it a formatted improv show like the Harold or the Deconstruction where you have an order of scenes, an idea of how many people should be on stage when, and beats for when characters from different scenes should come together? Is it thematic? If so, how is the theme used at different points of the show?

Write down your structure here.

Timing

You may need to have slightly different timings depending on the shows you get to perform. For Project2, we have shows of 15, 30, 45 and 60 minutes, so there is a difference in how we play with pacing and story for all of those.

Write down your timings here, including any modifications to your above structure for shorter or longer sets.

Number of players

As it says on the tin; how many are in your show and does it work with more or less? Have you tried it? We have eleven players in The Maydays, but shows normally have four to six players in them depending on the form we are using.

Put your smallest/ideal/largest number of players here:

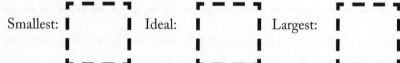

Smallest: Ideal: Largest:

The suggestion

This is more complicated than you would think. Project2 have been going for five years as I write this, and on Monday we changed how we get our call-out. Try a few and stick with the one or ones that work. It's a good idea to reverse-engineer what you want. In Project2 we discovered that we enjoyed specific locations for science fiction rather than big ones. Mars is a little too generic, but we loved Cloning Lab.

Here is a good process for working out your best ask-for.

Name ten of the *least* inspiring audience suggestions that you can imagine or have already had:

The ones I came up with regarding Project2 are broad. They don't narrow down the genre of science fiction for us. There are a million films set in a spaceship. We can do it but in order to get excited, we want more detail to launch us right into it. Jefferies tubes (maintenance conduits on the USS Enterprise) means that we get the Star Trek franchise too much in our heads and it becomes a reference-fest.

What do these have in common?

Name ten of the *most* inspiring audience suggestions that you can imagine or have already had:

What do these have in common?

They put us in mind of particular movies. They conjure an interesting stage picture. They make us think of using specific tools (like voiceover in the lift or many of the same character in a cloning lab). It's often fun having something banal or everyday, so that we can take it to the nth degree and show what would go wrong with it in the future or an alternative dimension. Endling, meaning 'the last of a species', gives us a mood and therefore a type of science fiction that it drives us into.

Hopefully you have an idea of what you want and what you don't want. Now you have to figure out how to ask for it! First of all, Project2 get the audience to shout out their favourite sci-fi book, comic, film or TV series, then we provide examples of big, small, real-world and time-travel locations such as:

> The Death Star in *Star Wars*.
> The meadow in *The Time-Traveller's Wife*.
> The egg incubator in *Jurassic Park*.

We've been broad enough that most people have a location in mind that they shout out. If they're attached to a franchise, we'll take that out of it. We can still use that world if we want to, but we are not contracted to it. Our world can end up different as long as we're in agreement with one another. If we did get the Death Star, we would rebrand it to 'a warship the size of a moon' or if we got the TARDIS we would say 'a time-travelling booth' or 'a phone box' (which might not time-travel). We always show our working by repeating the suggestion we heard and saying our version of it out loud.

Of course, Project2 do science fiction and that may be very different from your show. In our Tim Burton musical *Happily Never After*, The Maydays ask for a profession one of your grandparents had. This way, we get a profession that isn't too modern for our world and the call-outs tend to be more varied than the classic 'taxidermist' or 'gynaecologist' ones that'd we'd get asking for any profession.

Outside of a genre show, think of a new and interesting way of asking for 'a word'; one that begins with a particular letter, something you might find in a specific location or a word that you like the sound of.

Put your call-out here (with any scripted intro you need).

Scenes

Are there different types of scene in your show? Go ahead and define them and be clear about what you want from them. Are they group scenes, solos or twoprovs? Do you allow walk-ons in the first three scenes? Are your scenes slow-burn, fast and gaggy, naturalistic, truthful, competitive, pile-ons…

Now write a guide for these types of scene as I did with the Living Room.

Hey, here's a tick list but add as many as you can and tick the boxes that apply.

- ☐ Slow
- ☐ Group scenes
- ☐ Solo scenes
- ☐ Two-person scenes
- ☐ Walk-ons
- ☐ Fast
- ☐ Varying pace
- ☐ Mapping
- ☐ Game
- ☐ Cartoony characters
- ☐ Realistic/thin-veil characters
- ☐ Soap-opera emotion
- ☐ True-to-life emotion
- ☐ Split scene
- ☐ It's different every time

Add your own:

☐
☐
☐
☐

Edits

Edits are very important to the style of your show; they make it one thing or another. Tick the edits that apply to you and add your own.

☐   Tag-out
☐   Sweep
☐   Sliding door
☐   Self-edit
☐   Blackout
☐   Swarm
☐   Object
☐   'Flashback'
☐   I don't know what any of these are
    I know other edits that you have never heard of:

☐
☐
☐
☐

Other tips

By which I mean anything else that doesn't come under the above.

• What are you going to wear?

• Any furniture or props you need on stage?

• What are your boundaries with this group?

• Do you need paper, pens and a receptacle for people to put written suggestions before the show?

Warm-ups for this style

What aspects are there to this show?

If it's physical we'll need a stretch and something to get the heart pumping.

If it's heady, complex and full of wordplay and memory games we'll need to get the brain warmed up.

Is it silly? Then you'll need to get in the mood and start looking like an idiot now.

You have time for four warm-ups. Put the perfect four below:

1:

2:

3:

4:

Get everyone in the group to have a go at this and compile the best version of all your answers. Hopefully this will spark discussion on any points that still need work. If you have a coach, your conclusions may help them with the direction you are headed in.

This is not a contract that holds you to playing your show exactly like this. All improv should be free enough to go wherever the funny and the joy lives. You should never be on stage and feel annoyed that someone has broken 'the rules'. Afterwards, just look at that choice and see if it worked or not. This is just a short cut to defining a style and having a fun time within that world. It's also a great tool for newcomers and guests to your show.

Aces! You've made it to the end of Week Seven.

Let's go through our weekly practice checklist.

Read

Did you read the chapter? Well done!

Improvise

Form exercises

WHAT HAPPENS NEXT?

Have one of your team stand on the stage and ask:

"What happens first?"

Any of the team can give them a simple action like "You pick up a letter."

The actor will simply perform that action without adding anything. Then they say:

"What happens next?"

Give them another action. Give them fun things you would like to do! When you have given around ten instructions, or after a minute or two, you cannot add any more information to your instructions. That means if all you had mentioned was a letter, some ink, a chair and a cardigan, those are the only things they can use. It's a great exercise for recycling the things you already have and it automatically helps create a narrative story circle.

FREEFORM

Freeform or montage is a style where the show is – as you would imagine – structureless. It may adopt a structure or fall into an existing form as it goes along, but the players are not intending one. It can use any tools the players are familiar with. It's a great way to play with people with whom you have never performed or rehearsed before. I regularly play in freeform shows at festivals because although they require a lot of skill, they don't necessarily need rehearsal with one group of people like some other structures do.

GAME OF THE SHOW

Game of the Show is an extension of freeform. It starts without a structure or style but discovers itself in the making. Game of the Show is really about doubling-down on everything you have just done. If you edit by singing a song, that will be the style of edit from now on, if your first few characters are introduced by a butler, perhaps that's what happens for the rest of the show. Look at what you already have – and do more of it. If you play Game of the Show well, you might even end up with forms that you'd like to rehearse and perform again.

THREE IN A CIRCLE

Have one of your group step into the centre of the circle and announce that they are a particular thing.

"I am a lamb."

Someone else will step in with something that seems to fit with that.

"I am a farmer."

Then the third person will bring a third thing in that ties the other two together.

"I am Sunday lunch."

The first person (lamb guy) will then choose one of the others to remain and a new set of three will start.

"I choose the farmer."

"I am a farmer."

"I am a tree."

"I am a boundary dispute."

This warm-up exercise helps you identify patterns, groups, themes and connections. If you played this for a while, you'll find that the farmer or the lamb may come back and get a big reaction because it's happening at the 'right' time.

Find your own form

Why not create or find your own form? Play around with longform ideas that you find interesting and understand that it might take some rehearsal time before your show works.

The Maydays perform *Pitch That Show* which came out of a shortform game that I saw at the Edinburgh Fringe. We were at our Improv Retreat festival teaching and doing shows in beautiful Dorset and we wanted to create something different. I suggested making up show ideas based on two initials the audience gave us and having them vote for their favourite one. *Pitch That Show* is now one of our regular forms. A couple of nights ago the audience chose the initials JB and the winning pitch was Justice Boulevard. In this form, we meet lots of horrible characters in the first half and in the second half we see them get their comeuppance.

Find your own form exercise

Get everyone to come up with a form idea and try a bunch of them. If one is particularly fun or interesting, note what you liked about it and hone those ideas.

Game exercises

What?

Play a scene. At any point after the first few lines, one improviser says "What?" Both improvisers pause and retroactively add huge importance to the line before "What?"

It might go like this:

> PLAYER ONE: "I'm so excited to be pregnant."
> PLAYER TWO: "We're going to be the best parents."
> PLAYER ONE: "This room will look amazing pink."
> PLAYER TWO: "What?"
> *Pause.*
> PLAYER TWO: "Cynthia, do you know the gender of our child? I thought we agreed not to find out!"

The otherwise innocuous comment – "This room will look amazing pink" – becomes an example of trend in their relationship. The rest of the game can be other examples of where Cynthia has gone against an agreement they have made.

PLAYER ONE: "When the chaise longue arrives, we'll have somewhere to sit."

PLAYER TWO: "I thought we agreed that we would wait for Mum to take us out furniture shopping?!"

Slow-burn exercise

WHAT YOU JUST SAID IS VERY IMPORTANT TO ME BECAUSE...

In pairs, start every line with "What you just said to me is very important because..." It makes you listen much more carefully to every word in the line just before you speak. Don't worry about the larger context of the scene for this exercise; only concentrate on what they have JUST said and why that's important to YOU.

Genre exercise

GENRE CAULDRON (from Anthony Atamanuik's The Movie class)

Stand in a circle and name three movies which are in the same genre like *Alien*, *Moon* and *Sunshine*. Sing the phrase "Genre Cauldron" a few times before all calling out shots, character traits, typical lines, music choices, set and costume design, casting choices and so forth from the genre. When you run out, sing "Genre Cauldron" again!

Project2 start with a suggestion and play the first scene or two however we want. Based on these scenes we determine what kind of science-fiction story we are in. If it's a haunting 1970s-style one, we'll push into a slowburn style; if it's quick and gaggy then we'll drive harder into that, all the while using science-fiction tropes to define the subgenre.

Watch

Did you manage to see a show?

What was it?

Reflect

Write down your notes or thoughts on what you read, saw or did this week.

Week Eight:
Bad Gigs

This week we'll look at why some gigs just go badly. Sometimes it's our state of mind, our personal life, outside circumstances and so forth, but it's never fun to have a bad show. Let's think about that while I tell you about some of the awful shows that I have played.

A Bad Show

Most people have a great first show – I think because we don't actually know that much and we're just hoping we 'survive'. People worry that they'll reveal something personal on stage by mistake or completely blank or fall over when they enter – but none of that happens. On top of surviving, you get laughs and that feels amazing for the first time ever (or the first time in a new art form). You also tend to have a really supportive audience because they are friends and family who just want to see you do really, really well. Student shows are also often right after eight to twelve weeks of regular rehearsal and work. So there are a lot of factors on your side.

The more experienced you get, the more 'rules' you know about improv, so you are more aware of when you have done something you 'shouldn't have', like asked questions or forgotten a name or not followed your body when it wanted to edit. Perhaps you hardly even manage to get on stage. If you've come from a shortform background, it can feel weird that longform gives *you* – and not the director – all the control of how much you go on and when.

One of my students said that he felt 'due' for a bad show. Perhaps there's something in that. If we didn't have bad shows, it would indicate we were a poor judge of our work. You can still enjoy every show, but there is going to be a sliding scale. There will also be shows where you personally had a great one but where the whole show wasn't great or where the show was fantastic and everyone liked it, but you know you didn't do your best work. It was good in spite of you. I used to have really bad shows whenever my husband was in because I'd be worrying about whether he liked them.

Good gigs are fun, but bad ones are where you learn the most.

A Terrible Show

Well, there are no two ways about it: I had a terrible gig. For me it's not a hobby, it's my career. It cuts me to the quick to be bad at improv. At the same time, it's nice to be able to diagnose what I did wrong and re-learn the lessons that have got me through this stuff before.

Fear

I forgot the Bene Gesserit litany against fear (from the *Dune* books):

> **"I must not fear.** Fear is the mind-killer.
> Fear is the little-death that brings total obliteration.
> I will face my fear.
> I will permit it to pass over me and through me.
> And when it has gone past I will turn the inner eye to
> see its path.
> Where the fear has gone there will be nothing.
> Only I will remain."

Narcissism

I got all up in my head about me and how good or bad I was being and/or going to be. I didn't support my scene partners and I forgot to trust that they were looking out for me.

Warming up

My team have discussed in the past that it's not enough to have a chat or a burger, but that we need to play a handful of games to get on the same page. We even have a cache of games ready to go as 'our' warm-up, which serve the style and the philosophy of our work, and we just plain didn't do any of them this time.

Comparison

I saw another team earlier in the night and thought they were good. I worried that they were better than me. So they were.

Perception

A few people told me they really enjoyed the set and that it was super-fun. I could have taken the compliment, not invented reasons why they might have been lying to me or just being polite. They enjoyed it. They were right to have enjoyed it.

If I were my student, here is the advice I would give myself

Katy: I had a terrible gig.

Katy: Really? Why was that?

Katy: I just got up in my head and I fucked it.

Katy: Well, we all have bad gigs. Happily, the more experienced you get, the less they come up. You get a better hit-rate of good gigs the more improv gigs you do.

Katy: But it totally sucked and I want to die.

Katy: I often find that when I have a rough time in improv, it's because I have moved my own bar. A gig that I felt good about ten years ago might feel really poop today. I also often perceive that I have bad gigs for short periods when I am learning new things and trying to apply them. It's a good thing; it means I am learning.

Katy: I feel really awful about it. It makes me depressed.

Katy: You should never feel bad about a gig for longer than the gig took. I came across that in Pam Victor's article 'The Shoulda, Coulda, Woulda Game'.

Katy: I've already thought about it for way longer than it lasted.

Katy: Bad gigs mean that there is stuff to work on and that's what rehearsals are for. Make sure that you get together with your team right after a show and only share what you enjoyed about it. Later, in rehearsals, you can actively work on things to make the show better. Good shows are super-fun, but bad shows give you lots of great stuff to work on.

Katy: Thanks Katy, you're ace.

Katy: No worries, Katy. You're ace too. Stop being so hard on yourself.

[*Katy gives Katy a hug.*]

The Hardest Gig I Ever Played

Most people fear standing and performing in front of a crowd, most people fear not having the approval of their family and friends, and almost everyone fears death. The hardest gig I ever played was when my dad asked me to sing a comedy song at my mother's funeral.

There are two strands to this story. One is my mother's ovarian cancer and the other is comedy.

It was 2011 and I had only been in London a year. I was trying to put a comedy career together but at the time I was working in a soul-destroying job at Great Ormond Street Hospital where I would take cigarette breaks even though I didn't smoke. I would hula-hoop on the roof or cry in the toilets when things got too much. At the time, I thought it was just the job, but I was internalising my fear about my mother's illness.

My mum was amazing and she was ginger. There is a story that when she was in her twenties she caused a car crash because she was wearing very short shorts and a passing driver was staring at her legs. She believed that she was stupid because she was dyslexic. She was, in fact, super-smart. She made curtains and loose covers. Whenever we went out to restaurants she would lean over and check the lining of their curtains and tut. She was 5'2", but could rip apples in half with her bare hands. Mum had been ill and had recovered a couple of times. We all thought she was doing great. But this time, when she got the diagnosis again, there was a tone in her voice that told me this was the one that might win.

I got a casting; a really great casting for a TV role that I imagined was perfect for me. I absolutely believed I would get it and when I didn't (not even a recall), life at the NHS became one hundred per cent harder. I persuaded everyone else there to start hula-hooping with me.

My mum got increasingly ill until the point where she decided not to have treatment. She didn't want to spend the rest of her time feeling nauseous on the treatment and being a burden to others. I visited her every weekend or so for several months.

I had another casting. This one wasn't for a TV show, but for a profit-share sketch show called *NewsRevue*. I got it. I couldn't afford to do that show; it rehearsed Tuesday to Thursday with shows Thursday-Sunday. The rest of the time I would be writing and learning my lines. *NewsRevue* is a rolling satirical sketch show, so it was different week to week and often night to night. I had to take it, because I think I would otherwise have been crushed. So there I was, I had escaped! I had an amazing time. My brain was being used. I was writing comedy songs and sketches and making great new friends.

Then I got the call that my mum had passed away.

I was in rehearsal and stepped outside to take it. I didn't tell the cast. I emailed them all that night to say that the best thing I could do to get through that time was just to keep going. Not to talk about it in rehearsal, but to keep enjoying the show and not miss a single one.

Because I was writing all the time, the way I expressed grief was in a comedy song that I wrote on the ukulele for my mum the day after I found out she had died. If you don't know what a ukulele is, it's a substitute instrument for people who can't play a musical instrument. The chorus was about how she called herself 'ginger, short and dyslexic' but I rebranded it to 'auburn, petite and smart'. I recorded it and sent it to my dad who asked if he could play it at the funeral. I said yes but he insisted that I played it live.

It's tough doing stand-up at a funeral. How do you do a comedy song to sixty people including yourself who are literally crying? For me it was the hardest, longest few minutes of my life. I was trying to concentrate on breathing. My comedian persona kicked in as some kind of autopilot. My dad tells it back to me that I took to the stand and instead of just playing the song, I opened with "So, how's everyone doing? This is depressing, isn't it!" Not a clever or funny opening line, but it was truthful. It broke some of the tension and everyone laughed.

I'm glad my dad made me play the song, I'm glad that the last thing my mum knew about me was that I was following my dreams.

So even though you're not really supposed to, you should hula-hoop at the hospital and laugh at a funeral. Comedy is such a powerful tool and no matter how bad your last gig was, at least you're doing something you love.

I Want to Be Here Right Now

I was lucky enough to be working with Bill Arnett last January (Chicago Improv Studio/iO Chicago). Out of the many useful pieces of training and advice, this one sounded pretty great:

> "I want to be here right now. That's my only motive."
> Bill Arnett

That's the most essential thing to help you improvise. And easy, right? Nope.

I had a tough (read 'bad') show a few weeks back and we were trying to figure out what went wrong. We did a proper warm-up, there was a full room… We were doing consistently good shows and had been for a while, but then this stinker came out of nowhere.

We have a policy nowadays to say only good things after the show and be constructive with anything else in rehearsal. We lasted until the Tube before we started evaluating what made our improv slip: "We were on first, it was a weird room, the audience had never seen improv, the warm-up took the piss out of improv," and so forth. If a show's good it tends to cut through the things stacked against it, or at least *you* can appreciate that the show was good, even if the audience didn't like it.

Having recently heard Bill's wisdom, I wondered if I wanted to be at that show right then. I had definitely wanted to be there when I arrived, but one of my show buddies called in sick and the other was disappointed by that and had been partying till 8 a.m. I jokingly told my partner that I did not have his back, but on reflection I wonder if I was joking? (Also, shit joke, Katy.) Perhaps I was mad that he was disappointed in only having me to play with and that he hadn't slept. I felt like I was going to have to 'carry' him, which made it seem like work and not fun.

All you have to do is want to be there.

I was blaming him for not wanting to be there which made me not want to be there. Newsflash: neither of us wanted to be there. What if you don't want to be there and you have to do a show anyway? You can't drop out of a show just because the vibe isn't right!

We normally suggest one personal mission before the show like "I'm going to be silly", "I'm going to play emotional honesty", "I'm going to do some ridiculous characters", "I'm going to use the space well", and so forth. Then we all take on the missions as a group and that often determines the style and pace of that evening's show. We forgot to do our missions. Our missions should have been "I'm going to treat you like an artist, a poet and a genius", "I'm going to make you laugh", "I'm going to use this weird space in wonderful ways." My advice to you and future me is: want to be there – or fake it till you make it and make sure you treat your scene partner like a legend. There is no carrying, there is only improv, which is your favourite thing to do.

This applies to bigger casts too. Everyone is there to play the whole show. Take note if you ever decide just to be the walk-on guy because you're a bit tired, or ill, or hungover. It's not okay to just be comedy walk-on guy unless that's exactly what the show needs you to do at the time. You can't decide beforehand. You have to be there to serve the whole show and whatever is needed in that show. What if everyone decides to be comedy walk-on guy? That'll be a shit show.

It's not okay to announce you'd rather be somewhere else, or you don't like the show you're doing, because that stops other people wanting to be there and play with you.

I definitely want to be here right now – and for the rest of my life.

Strategies for wanting to be here
- Remind yourself of why you're doing improv, why you want to play with these people and what you can do to give them a good time. (If you don't feel good about those people and that show, you'll need to address that and think about leaving the group or dealing with the issues you may have.)

- Treat shows with respect. Turning up without enough sleep or with a terrible hangover makes everyone else have to work harder on your behalf.
- If you know in advance that you'll be tired or overbusy, it might be best to say you're unavailable for the show.
- Fake it till you make it. Play a character that is very excited to be playing in an improv show! It won't take long to remember that's who you really are.
- I find that having a special costume or outfit for a show puts me right back into show mode when I put it on.
- Make sure you've eaten! Hungry players aren't always the best players!
- Hydrate!
- Throw out all your stresses and concerns before the warm-up. Have everyone go into the centre of the circle and shout them out. After each one shout "Suck My Dick" and then change who goes in the middle. Shannon O'Neill taught me this one. With everything out of the way, you can get into an improv mind-set.
- Play everyone's very favourite warm-up so that you can rekindle the fun!
- Having a warm-up that is an established ritual can be helpful in achieving that familiar show head-space too.
- Warm up properly even if it feels awkward or you don't have a special room for it. I have done warm-ups in the toilets, outside in the snow and silently at the back of crowded pubs.
- Stand like Wonder Woman. It will give you a boost of testosterone to make you feel more confident about going on stage.

Nice one! You've made it to the end of Week Eight.

Let's go through our weekly practice checklist.

Read

Did you read the chapter? I reckon!

Improvise

This week, take a break from improv and do these tasks instead:

Be a beginner at something.

Try a hobby of some kind that you've never done before.

Reflect for five minutes on how far you've come since your first improv class.

Hang out with your team. Social time with your group can make your improv improve purely because you know each other better and care for one another more.

If you want to pretend it's still work, go and see a play or a movie for inspiration. If you just want to bond, do karaoke, go bowling, do mini-golf or something else…

Watch

Did you manage to see a show?

What was it?

Reflect

Write down your notes or thoughts on what you read, saw or did this week.

Week Nine:
Recovering

In improvisation, it's much easier to get on board with someone who is enjoying themselves and playing as if what they said or did is excellent. Don't apologise but accept that failing is a huge part of improvisation and it is low-cost. The worst thing that can happen really is that the audience or your fellow players will laugh and that's often the response you are going for! We expose ourselves to a lot of self-criticism and occasionally forget to enjoy the moment where what we have played or suggested works and is appreciated by someone else. Sell your ideas and get used to people enjoying them.

Audience Versus Improviser

It seems to me that there is sometimes quite a disparity between how much an audience enjoys a show and how much the performers do.

For me, there are three broad reactions I'll have after doing a show.

- Recriminating myself for being awful (though I'm a lot kinder to myself these days).
- Fairly satisfied, but analysing the hell out of the show ("Mr Muscle was a funny character, but why didn't we have any depth to our relationships?").
- An air-punch where it was so great that I love my life and the show and everyone I've ever met (I like the term 'way-homer' for these; where you keep remembering a great moment from your show all the way home).

There's a reaction around the ego where you personally feel you did or didn't do good work. Sometimes it can feel like you're the only one who dropped the ball, or the only one who kept it together. In improv, if the show as a whole fails, you feel like you've failed because it's a team game. Conversely, sometimes a show can fail because one person stood out and the whole team game fell apart. Your job is to make other people look good.

With shortform there are in-built safety nets and that's why many students start there. If you are brand-new you will likely succeed because of these reasons:

- The audience are probably your friends and family.
- Games automatically generate jokes and let the audience know when to laugh. For example, the game NEW CHOICE gives you a 'set-up, set-up, twist' joke structure that nearly always works.
- The audience love to see you die just as much – if not more – than they like to see you succeed. In DIE, STORYTELLER, DIE, a competitive storytelling game, the audience shouts: "Die!" when you mess up the story. If no one died, the game wouldn't be fun.

With longform it's a little harder because there is less tolerance of bad improv. There aren't built-in safety nets (unless you count a form you're using, but that's really just a structure). If you are just truthful and listen well, the audience are much more keen to see that than you being clever or funny, but it does take years and years for people to feel perfectly comfortable doing those simple things on stage.

Coming offstage it's sometimes confusing having the audience really love a show that you thought was bad or okay. When someone comes up to you to tell you how great your show was, don't tell them that they're wrong! Telling a fan of your show that they are incorrect or that your show is poor makes them feel stupid. Just say thank you and work on your craft. Remember that they might be right and you might be wrong.

There seem to be a couple of reasons for the disparity between the audience and improviser's viewpoints. Audiences might not have seen as much improv as you. Some people are pretty amazed that you can make up a show as you go and they thoroughly enjoy the magic unfolding.

For me, I feel like a show fails when I am consciously working hard on it on stage. Improvisers call this 'being in your head'. My favourite of the shows I have done are where my characters feel like they are being channelled and have a life of their own, that the beats or chapters of the narrative naturally fall out one by one. I am perfectly in the group mind of the company and we all have similar ideas and initiations, or immediately enjoy and jump on board with the surprises. So, what's the difference between one of those shows and one where I am standing on the side thinking, "I haven't really done many characters, maybe I'll do a character?" Well, here's my revelation: nothing. Nothing from the audience's perspective. For them, it's a great show. They enjoyed everything about it. It just happens that today, your autopilot didn't kick in as well and you had to fly on manual.

I had a show after Christmas one year when I hadn't done a show for a few weeks. I thought, "Ah, it'll be fine – I've been doing improv for years." Even if you're an Olympic diver, you can't just fall off the board and expect it to work – you have to use all your awareness and training and make that dive happen. That post-Christmas show was a belly flop. If you have a show where some other part of your brain is doing all the work, lucky you. I'm not suggesting you spend all your time on stage consciously planning and analysing; I am suggesting that you need to be alert and open the whole time. You can't just sit back and expect it all to happen.

There might also be shows where you loved it but the audience didn't. It was your best work, you did great but the audience disengaged. These shows tend to disappear after you've done a fair bit of improv, but the causes can be vanity and in-jokes. If you're doing all your best schtick and having a super time, but not listening to the other players, you may feel you did a great show, but the audience probably felt the gap between you and the other players. You might have something that you do in rehearsals, but the audience are not only going to miss the joke but feel distanced by it. The other possibility, of course, is that it wasn't the right audience for your show. Have a check-in at your next rehearsal and see how the group feels.

It's great to know what you're working on. It's the only way your improv will get better. Enjoy the things you did well just as much as you notice the stuff you want to build on. You are doing this because you love it (no one chooses improv as a sure-fire career path), so notice the great bits. I used to keep a file on my laptop; every time someone said something nice about me or my team's improv, I would make a note of it. That way, if I had a terrible show or thought my work sucked, I could have a look back and realise that I was probably just forgetting to give myself positive notes as well as constructive ones.

Remember that improv is a team sport. Everyone has your back. The team win – you win! Hell, that's why I benched stand-up to do more improv. And it's okay to fly on manual sometimes. It won't feel quite as magical as those autopilot gigs, but unless you show the effort on your face, your secret is safe: the audience won't be able to tell the difference.

Don't Congratulate Yourself Too Much or Berate Yourself Either

Years ago, when I wrote the first version of this, I had just had three fantastic reviews for Katy and Rach, Music Box *and* The Maydays…

Before I celebrate, let's remember Baz Luhrmann's track 'Everybody's Free (To Wear Sunscreen)' offering advice to college leavers:

> "Whatever you do, don't congratulate yourself too much
> or berate yourself either."

Careful if you listen to it, though – it always makes me cry. You can go on too much of an ego roller coaster if you're not careful and that's why a lot of comics and performers become depressive or alcoholic. One night people think you're great and the next people think you're not. So, are you great? Or shit?

Reviews are hard to ignore. A bad review can curb your audience numbers. For my first directorial experience at the Edinburgh Festival Fringe, the *Scotsman* reviewer gave us one star. The review described my cast as 'rampaging toddlers' and despite flagging it as a great idea for a show, and pointing out 'an impressive backwards farce skit', we were damned. I remember the first line clearly, though it was around seventeen years ago: "This is the hell that is student theatre." I had to take my cast to one side before the next show and explain to them that it was one person's opinion and that if they believed it was a one-star show, then it was certainly going to come across like a one-star show. To add insult to injury, we failed to get any other reviews for the whole festival and therefore our *Scotsman* diatribe was the only voice out there. If we'd had another terrible review, at least it would be consolidated. If we'd had a good review, we could understand that people have different tastes or perhaps we'd caught the *Scotsman* on a bad day or a bad show. The cast went on to be on the Channel 4 *Big Breakfast* spot 'Edinburgh Cringe', and I was too sore to be a part of it. At the tender age of twenty, it was a big blow.

Criticism just makes you upset, whereas constructive criticism makes you happy because you can see a way to make your show better. "Yes," you think; "that bit didn't work and now I can see that if the audience understood Clive's motivation, then it would be a stronger piece."

A good bit of therapy for dealing with bad reviews is to review the review. Take apart the reviewer's language and point of view. It's always nicer to be part of a group for reviews – being part of an improv troupe instead of a lone stand-up, for example. One of my favourite reviews of all time was a two-star *Three Weeks* review for The Maydays' first show at the Edinburgh Fringe in 2006. We created a new form that played and then mashed together many shortform games. The reviewer summed it up as "reused drama workshop games". She wasn't wrong – I mean, that is the root of modern shortform improv (thanks, Viola Spolin and Keith Johnstone). Over the next few weeks, we thoroughly enjoyed describing Richard Alston dance as: "Just a bunch of people keeping fit"; comedian Rhod Gilbert as: "Just a bloke doing a bunch of jokes"; and cabaret legend Camille O'Sullivan as: "Just a woman singing with some people on musical instruments." Incidentally, Chortle came to the same exact show and gave us a glowing four-star review that we quoted on our publicity.

This is all very well, you say, but you started this with: "I got three fantastic reviews." Yes, but I hope to be no more affected by high praise than I am by being rubbished on paper. I have a good idea about what was wrong with all of these highly praised shows and they are things that we strive to improve continually. There will never be a point in improv when you are done.

Even *TJ and Dave*, *Baby Wants Candy* and all my favourite shows vary in quality and as an improviser that is satisfying in a way. If your show feels safe, it probably isn't that great. If you're not pushing boundaries then why are you improvising? If you're wheeling out your five favourite characters for the umpteenth time then why don't you write a script for them? The magic of improv lies in risk. If you're lucky, your risks will pay off and you'll get a good review. If not, well done you for expanding your range and striving for something better.

My advice is that if you want to get ecstatic about five-star reviews, you have to be depressed about one-star reviews, and your ego isn't worth all that trauma. In my opinion, we didn't deserve a five-star review for Saturday's Music Box show, but I also believe that we have done some brilliant five-star shows that weren't reviewed. I'm very pleased that we get to use that review to tell people how good we can be. I don't feel like we can sit back and enjoy that we're perfect. Still, I might quietly crack open a beer...

"Remember the compliments you receive, forget the insults; if you succeed in doing this, tell me how."
Baz Luhrmann – Everybody's Free (To Wear Sunscreen)

Conscious Incompetence (and Why It's Your Friend)

Over years of teaching improv, I have begun to notice that many students at one point or another appear to have a crisis of confidence and dips in their skill sets. There is an ongoing cycle that starts with enthusiasm, becomes more of a serious work ethic and then turns into a mini freak-out. I have always advised these students – based on observation – that a dip in confidence seems to come along at the same time or just before a big jump-up in skills. I had no evidence or explanation for this apart from my own observations. Until now.

I was working in Chantilly, France, coaching improvisational thinking with corporate leaders, and was struck by something one of the other coaches mentioned. If you work in the corporate world, this is probably not news to you, but it really lit up a light bulb for me. Noel Burch developed the Conscious Competence Ladder in the 1970s. There is a scale that runs like this:

> Unconscious incompetence
> Conscious incompetence
> Conscious competence
> Unconscious competence

First, we don't know that we can't do something, then we know we aren't doing it right, so then we learn to do it, then we forget that we're even doing it. For me, these are very clear levels within our improvisational learning. The most important of which is conscious incompetence.

When you are a total beginner in improv, you can often hugely enjoy performing; there are no nerves, no stress, you know you can do whatever you want and there's nothing important riding on it. You perform, you get *laughs* – which is amazing – and then you're done. Fun. After a while, you realise that you are maybe hitting on similar characters and gags because you know they work and because they feel easy and comfortable. You begin to realise that there's more to improv. Where is the initial spark you had, why has it got harder? There is more to learn. You look at the people around you and see that they have skills you don't, or that you're not as good at. So you work on those skills. You increase your range, you take more risks, you are starting to enjoy the work again. You get a lot better, then it's easy, then you are slightly disconnected. You're maybe the best person in your company and you start to feel frustrated that others can't keep up, or that the beginners' class is too easy for you; you are consciously competent. You join a more advanced class and really enjoy the scenes; they are rich, you are all listening to each other, and the audience likes your shows. You believe that this is the norm. You are no longer stressing about your skill level because it is comfortable. You have forgotten your struggle. You are unconsciously competent. You are *good*.

Oh wait, another group came to town. How the hell are they doing the improv they are doing? What is longform? Is that monologue genuinely from real life? Their physicality is incredible. They sing! Here we go again. Alexis Gallagher always maintains that it is best to be the second-worst person in a company. I think that's a nice way to aspire to good improv. That way, you are always consciously incompetent and trying to learn the skills you see around you. You're not the worst, though, so you're not going to feel like crap. Confidence is a key part of successful improv.

This is by no means an experience that is only applicable to beginners. I come across these blocks in my work every so often when I'm working with amazingly tight companies, strong singers and improvisers who never forget a name or drop a ball. Just remember, whenever you know that you are terrible, that your improv is stale, that your work sucks, that you are the least funny/interesting person on stage – that is the point where you can go up a level. That is the point where you're challenging yourself and taking risks. If you know you're the most funny, interesting, talented, spontaneous person in the room, change rooms. It's important to feel good about conscious incompetence. It's the point where you're most likely to surprise yourself, to take big risks and to push up your skill level.

Your degree of competence is important to different people in different ways:

The audience

Audiences love to watch people who are at their ease, even if those players are enjoying their own incompetence.

Your peers

Your fellow improvisers, employers and teachers; they all want you to be good. They want you to step up and they want to help you achieve great things. They also have your back.

Yourself

No one is a harsher judge than yourself. Enjoy it. Let you be the harsh critic of you. Just don't let the critic get in there when you're playing. Love a show, get out of your head. Then sit down after and watch the video, see what you did good and bad and set yourself some goals.

Now stand up and declare: "I am consciously incompetent" – and enjoy how much you can improve every time those words ring true.

Loving Your Crew

There seems to be a pattern to the life of an improvisation group.

- Meet at a regular class (or existing friends that take classes together).
- Some stay to continue practice.
- A few leave when performing becomes more of a focus than practising.
- A few leave when the show starts to develop into something new.
- The group is too small.
- One person resents doing all the admin.
- The group recruits new members.
- There is a split experience level.
- The show starts to develop into something new.

Then the last few points kind of cycle over time; people leave, people join, the show morphs and changes. This isn't always true, of course, there are groups of lifelong chums and there are shows that audition on Day One, following the vision of a director or coach. Largely, though, this is my experience in teaching and coaching teams and these cycles are stressors that influence the group's dynamic.

The Maydays are twelve years old, retaining two completely original members that were in the very first show. I joined within six months and others came at various intervals over the years. We lost people to commitment issues, personal gripes, artistic disagreement, success elsewhere, musical improv, relationships, moving overseas and many other things. We gained members through auditions, spotting talent in our classes, playing with people in other groups and so forth.

All of this is normal. A lot of groups – like new businesses – fail in the first year. People have different goals and there is also a point where all the fun of improv can get serious. Whether it's a group that has formed for fun or with some professional goal in their sights, ambition and drive can sometimes take the joy out of our art form. When we want to get it right, it can be hard to enjoy failing.

This section is my sticking plaster. I have done these exercises with various groups when they have forgotten the fun, including my own.

Book a rehearsal way in advance that everyone can make and impress upon everyone that it's like a family wedding and you really have to be there no matter what else is happening in your diary. Bring paper and pens.

Good job! You've made it to the end of Week Nine.
Let's go through our weekly practice checklist.

Read

Did you read the chapter? Nice one!

Improvise
Audience versus improviser exercise

- Keep a note of all the positive feedback you get. Write it on paper and put it in a jar. Save it for those times when you feel bad about your work and read as many as you need before you feel better!

Loving your crew exercise
PART ONE

1. Everyone write down one or two of your favourite improv warm-ups, each on a little square of paper. They don't have to be useful or something that anyone else likes. They can be the stupidest or most technical warm-ups in the world. The important thing is that you personally love them. When someone else gets you to play them, they make you really happy! So I might write down 'Hot Spot' and 'Mind Meld', which continue to be two of my favourites. Put all of the folded warm-ups in a hat or a jar or a pile. If you're a solo improviser, you should do this exactly the same way, just put a few more in the pot.

2. Everyone write down one or two of your favourite exercises on squares of paper and put them into another container or pile. For exercises, you could pick clear directions given at the top of open scenes (like eye contact or finding the game), shortform games or anything else that is more than a warm-up.

3. Now we mix the warm-ups together in their pile and the exercises together in their pile. The whole next part of rehearsal is working through these. Start with doing *all* of the warm-ups. You don't need to do them again if they come up

more than once, but it is delightful when you find that someone else has the same favourites as you!

4. Go ahead and play *all* of the exercises. Throw yourself at the ones you don't like (if there are any) because they are someone else's favourites. You don't each have to do every game, but make sure you get a go at the ones you put in the pot.

5. When you're through, I'm going to guess that you had a really great time! Get a cuppa and discuss what you enjoyed about all of that. Sometimes we forget just what we love about improv. We can get too serious; especially a few years in. When Project2 did this, we discovered that we still loved doing ridiculous shortform games and felt guilty about that; like they were lesser art. We were much more physical than normal and had more *fun*. Because there's no sense in the randomised structure and there is no pass or fail, only 'do it', we had a really great time.

6. Decide what you'd like to keep from this as a team. Remember how much you like to be physical or wordy or sing or mess stuff up or look like an idiot.

Part Two

For Brits, this next bit is hard, but maybe it's just how we are at taking compliments. Everyone takes a big bit of paper, writes their own name at the top and titles three categories:
- Things I love about your work
- Things I have learned from you
- Why I love playing with you

Take the time to write something under each category on everyone's sheet. Put some tunes on in the background. Your comments should be anonymous.

When you have written on everyone's sheet, get your own page back. Now – one at a time – sit in front of the others and read your sheet out loud. Other than reading, you are not allowed to offer any other comment than "Thank you". Make sure everyone gets a go.

We often forget why we do what we do. We forget how lucky we are to be playing with these particular amazing people. There might be one person you don't get on with as much or know as well as the others. I bet there's even something you have learned from them and a reason that you (even sometimes) really enjoy being in scenes together.

Keep that bit of paper in your jar of compliments. Remember that you are valued. This exercise is worth doing at least once or twice a year as we all change and grow in our work.

Watch

Did you manage to see a show?
What was it?

Reflect

Write down your notes or thoughts on what you read, saw or did this week.

Week Ten:
Community

Improv is about making other people look good, so this week is about how to take the philosophy of improv and apply it to the community outside of your actual shows and classes. As humans and artists we regularly fear missing out, we come up against jealousy and being treated with less than respect. Let's reach out and be better improvisers by being better people.

Fear of Missing Out

I used to feel sad when I wasn't asked to be in stuff, but then I realised that people aren't always thinking about me! On asking, people also assume that I'm constantly busy. Sometimes I am, sometimes I'm not. I've done well from just sucking up my pride and asking when there's something I want to be involved in. I was sad I didn't get asked to do a particular show, but I just emailed them and said it was a great project and I'd be happy to help out if they needed me. I was surprised to discover I was on the list of people they would like to use later in the run. Rather than getting bitter about it, I just said hi and told them how much I liked the idea. A chum was also sore about not being in more shows and she asked why she was never in *Geekeasy* (the Project2 comedy night for nerds). My response: "What? I had no idea you were interested, come play!" The advice is: if you like a show, just say you're excited to see it and if they ever need another player, you'd love to jump in.

For example, I don't get asked to do the annual *Fifty-Hour London Improvathon*. The year I wanted to do it, I asked to play and I was welcomed. Why should they keep a hundred improvisers in their heads? People we regard as 'names' in improv often ask to do it. Also, consider if this really is your type of thing. Do you enjoy it, or do you feel like you *should* do it because it's a kind of career move or networking opportunity? Don't do it if it feels like you *should*, do it if you think it would be fun.

It is good to be picky. Appreciate when you have space and downtime, because it's great to reflect and prioritise. Soon you'll go through a busy time again. Make a plan of how many nights you'd like to rehearse and do shows, then keep that time free until you find or create the right project. In acting and improv land, things often come along with no warning and it's good to be available. Sometimes I find that I'm just busy for the sake of being busy, or I miss an opportunity to do something I'd really like to do because I've committed to something I'm half interested in.

I don't think it's helpful to compare ourselves to one another. You just have to do things that excite you and push your improv in the direction that you want to go. I used to struggle to be validated in our improv community, but now I just do nerd stuff that makes me happy. *Who Ya Gonna Call?* was a *Ghostbusters* musical that I made with some friends. It had the remit of being an Edinburgh show just for fun while us cast were all doing 'real' projects up there. It turned out to be one of the most successful Edinburgh shows I've ever done and I think I'd done ten years at the Fringe before that. *Geekeasy* was just for kicks with my buds and a happy bonus when it led to other stuff. You might be able to reverse-engineer those opportunities, but it's very hard work and the opposite of following your joy.

Remember, everyone has neuroses about being excluded. Different people have just created different coping mechanisms. I read a great article recently which pointed out that when we are feeling anxious, we put in more work and more stress to try and solve it. Actually, it is suggested that the best cure is to sit back, let the anxiety pass and stop trying to do things about it. Relax, you're on the right path.

Jealousy

"It's better to be inspired by people than in competition with them."
Shannon O'Neill (UCB)

As well as the fear of missing out, there is jealousy. We're not only worried about missing out, but also venomous towards the person who does get to be involved. Jealousy is an odd one in improv because our whole philosophy is to make the other person look good. Unfortunately, we're always going to be scuppered by our egos. If I'm feeling jealousy towards a person I ask myself what it is that I am really jealous of. It's rarely the person and more likely to be something to do with a perceived failure in me.

My friend became a theatre director. He was the year below me at university and a very talented chap. I noted a few years after graduating that he was directing a show in London at a reputable theatre and shortly after that became their resident Artistic Director. I felt a pang of jealousy. I had wanted to be a theatre director since I was a kid. I wrote and directed my first play at college when I was seventeen.

I asked myself:

Who or what has prompted the jealousy?
My friend from uni.

Do I want that particular job?
(Very specifically 'that' job. Do I want to be directing that show at that theatre for that money?)
No.

Why/Why not?
Because I'm not interested in the plays that he is directing.

What aspect of it do you like?

The job of directing.

What would you like to do?

Direct one of my own shows.

What's stopping you?

(No 'time' or 'money' bullshit. Make time by getting up earlier or dropping other commitments, find a cheaper way of doing it or raise money. If you won't do those things, you don't want it bad enough. And if it's a big thing, there is always a smaller version you can do to get you started.)

Nothing is really stopping me.

What can I learn from him?

He did a directing postgraduate degree and did lots of work for free before he got this job.

Action plan

Get a bunch of friends together and direct a new show.

Often, the answer to 'Do I want that?' is 'no' and then the jealousy seems to evaporate. When it is 'yes', you can still find a way through. Action is the best cure for jealousy.

Because of this particular sting of jealousy, I directed an improv show that I was really proud of called *Silly String Theory*. I don't think it was purely because of this pang, but it was a catalyst. I did two full-time weeks of rehearsal with no pay for me or my cast (though I did try for funding) then put on six nights at a local theatre. It completely scratched that itch and I learned a lot. I got to do exactly the kind of work that I couldn't see anyone else doing in the UK and that I was excited about. We worked on truth, subtext, realism, Sondheim-style songs and scene-painting.

Are you jealous of anyone at the moment, or is there something that springs to mind from the recent past?

Answer the same questions

Who or what has prompted the jealousy?

Do you want that particular job/thing?

Why?/Why not?

What aspect of it do you like?

What would you like to do?

What's stopping you (no 'time' or 'money' bullshit)?

Anything you can learn from it/him/her?

Action plan

Rather than spending your energy on hate or entitlement, be active. Jealousy is a misappropriation of ambition, drive and focus. It's as if your boat was sinking and you were using all your power to swim downwards instead of to the shore. Jealousy can show you career goals, courses of action and people who can help. Try not to get wrapped up in timelines. If a twenty-two-year-old has achieved something you wanted and you're forty, it shouldn't matter. If you spend five years resenting them for doing it, you won't be any closer to achieving it yourself. If you are envious of someone who can play the piano, stop wasting your time and energy hating that person and start learning the fucking piano.

Superchickens

From a TED talk by Margaret Heffernan:

"An evolutionary biologist at Purdue University named William Muir studied chickens. He was interested in productivity... but it's easy to measure in chickens because you just count the eggs. He wanted to know what could make his chickens more productive, so he devised a beautiful experiment. Chickens live in groups, so first of all, he selected just an average flock, and he let it alone for six generations. But then he created a second group of the individually most productive chickens – you could call them superchickens – and he put them together in a superflock, and each generation, he selected only the most productive for breeding. After six generations had passed, what did he find? Well, the first group, the average group, was doing just fine. They were all plump and fully feathered and egg production had increased dramatically. What about the second group? Well, all but three were dead. They'd pecked the rest to death. The individually productive chickens had only achieved their success by suppressing the productivity of the rest."

The other side of jealousy

Let's look at the other side of jealousy too. When you're the person someone else is jealous of, it can be unpleasant. It's hard to turn off jealousy, particularly in those first few moments, but don't forget to celebrate the success for that other person. They don't want to spend their moment of glory commiserating you. Let them enjoy it. If you want to think selfishly about it, having successful friends in the same field makes you more likely to be successful yourself. A rising tide lifts all ships.

I was discussing this with a friend and she said that in order to win, you must just get better than the other person. I disagree. I say be happier and then you won't even be thinking about it.

Stop Gender-Casting Your Improv Show

I hope that in being honest about my opinions, we can have an open discussion about women not just playing women in improv.

More and more I hear people say that they have asked the women in their improv show to just play women and the men to just play men. The reasoning is normally "to make it more like theatre". In my experience I have only seen men make this decision. When we start calling 'theatre' an excuse for casting improv a certain way, it makes me sad.

One of the things that I find the most fun and rewarding about being an improviser is that we are not hampered by our casting. By casting, I mean what people assume about you the moment they look at you. That is about age, gender, race and also how you dress. If I go to a casting for a commercial, I'm only ever going to be able to play what I look like. Right now, I'm thirty-six with a blonde frizzy bob and 1950s cat-eye Ray-Bans. I'm a slightly pear-shaped size ten with a weak chin currently having my teeth put in a straight line. Recently I have played a school teacher, a wife/mother, the voice in someone's head, a peasant, a queen, a presenter and an antiques dealer. All of those have been comedy roles because of the quirky girl-next-door comedy face I have. I won't be cast as American because of my still-working-on-it teeth; I won't be cast as male because I'm female; and I won't be cast as ages that are much different than my own. Unless or until I become a 'name' it's unlikely I'll be cast outside of my actual physical appearance on screen.

Perhaps because of my casting, one of the things I adore in improv is that I can play anyone. I can change my posture and movement to give the impression of a different body, I can play the beauty, the man, the very old and the very young. I can play a lamp if I want to, or a concept, or a farm animal. I once improvised the bridge of a song as a turd floating in a jacuzzi.

There is also lack of diversity in the London improv scene that all of the improv theatres and schools are working to change. Perhaps someone can speak to that from experience in the same way I can talk about my gender and certainly it's up to those of us making and casting shows to be inclusive.

Surprisingly I often hear the argument that the audience 'will not understand' that a man is playing a woman or a woman is playing a man. If you are clear with the names you use, the physicality you adopt and so forth, the audience will definitely come with you. The same people who cast shows gender-appropriately do not often have people play their own age or their own appearance, so why is gender the one element that gets enforced? Play to the top of your intelligence and don't patronise the audience. If we really don't get the fact that a man is playing a women the first time, it will be an education and the next time around we will all be smarter.

I watched a show recently that was cast with women only playing women and men only playing men. The director is one of my best (male) chums and is a feminist. It is a show with many historically-set scenes. As you can imagine, the story contained a lot of incidences of women being repressed throughout civilised culture and the women always played the subordinate, weak roles. This might have been a feminist commentary, but sadly, every single female interaction always mentioned men, relationships with men and sex with men. If you are not aware of the Bechdel test, now is a good time to look it up. There was no scene where women were talking exclusively about anything other than men for more than a line or two. In the one scene where I did see a woman taking charge of the scene and reframing in favour of the woman, I was sad to see it switched back (and denied) by the man in the scene. I don't think that casting choice helped the show and actually made the innate sexism of the ages fall back into the present day. The director commented, "I believe that playing your own gender expression creates theatre of heightened authenticity."

As part of Slapdash Festival a few years ago, I took part in a really fun John Hughes improv show that was cast with women only playing women and men only playing men. The men got to be the bike-riding fun-having college teens and the women got to be the girls obsessed with those men. Yes, that is honouring the genre, but I really don't think it would have been a struggle to play across gender and have the audience come with us. After all, we were all in our thirties and forties playing teenagers and half of us were Brits playing Americans.

> "Also, you can do history that is better than history and John Hughes that is better than John Hughes. If being a woman is something unsavoury to play, there's something else to fix."
> Jill Bernard (in response to my blog)

My third example of this trend is from a corporate job I did recently where we enacted The Dream. In this short format, you ask for the real-life experiences of an audience member and then show them the dream or nightmare that they might have that night. Before the show there was a debate about who could or should play the audience member. I argued that any one of us that had an idea or felt the urge should step up to play them or it should fall out organically. Others (including the other woman in the cast) felt that the audience wouldn't be able to cope with the fact that a man might be playing a woman, or a woman a man. I believe that if you use their name in the first instance it's easy to know who they are, and if that's too hard – they are the protagonist of the story you just heard! Go figure! People aren't stupid. If they are, educate them. Treat the audience as poets and geniuses.

Please let us educate our audiences and our directors. Let's enjoy the full range of make 'em ups and be able to play whoever and whatever we please.

In improv, I can play a cat, a sunset or a five-year-old, so why can't I play a man?

Please also take a look at the article *Gender in Improv – A Trans Perspective* by London-based Canadian improviser Stephen Davidson. Stephen asks why gender should come into it as much as it does. Does everything and everyone we play need to be defined in that way?

I also enjoyed talking to New Zealand improviser Christine Brooks about this. She suggests that we should play *more* women in improv and really work on our characters being rounded, having agency and caring about one another. Rather than just playing male archetypal roles, let's spend the time actively celebrating the diverse roles of women and their representations in art.

Another result of publishing the above as a blog was that a friend of mine told me about his gender-cast show. He's super-great, but we definitely disagreed on this point. He was making a show with all the character clichés of a horror movie: the slut, the jock, the nerd and so forth, but he wanted it to look right. In order to counter the gender argument, he wanted the cast to play their given gender, but the roles were flexible. So a man could play the slut and the woman the jock. I pointed out that a man cannot play a slut. Society's guide for a woman who sleeps around is that she is a slut, that she's easy and that she's stupid. Society's guide for a man being a slut is… well, he's not a slut: he's a stud. He is more successful and sexy than the men around him and he's charismatic and smart. So you can't have a male slut. The jock male (accordingly to this genre) is highly regarded among his friends: he's competitive, a bully, physically strong and straight. Women are not called jocks. Women who are at the top of their field of sport are thought of (in this genre) as masculine and lesbian, and they would never have as big a part in a horror film as a jock male. So what this (male) director was doing was trying to make the theatricality more believable for an audience by having people play their own gender, but then asking them to get on board with something much more difficult: that a man can be a slut and a woman a jock in this genre – whilst still hitting the horror tropes in a simple way.

I am very interested in the idea of playing these parts in a new way but not at the cost of being cast by our bodies. Why not give everyone the choice? Allow a man to play a female slut, have a woman play a male jock, have a man play a male virgin who gets killed by the monster/insaniac. We create a lot of new possibilities when we play what we want. I don't have a problem with everyone playing their own genders the whole time, but I don't want a director to make that decision for them. I want them to choose, and to be able to take the risk of it not working too.

The reason for the casting 'rule' (what a yucky word!) was for brevity. If we had more time to rehearse three-dimensional cross-gender characters then I would not have suggested it, but I felt that particularly the male portrayals of female stereotypes was blunt and there was little character depth. In hindsight I could and should have tackled this a different way, but time was against me and it was super-important to get the audience invested in these characters quickly so that they cared whether or not they lived or died.

The second thing was that I absolutely agree that the 'slut' is not easily transferable to men for the reasons you mentioned. However, we adjusted our own understanding of this archetype and it became 'the socialite' – someone who is mega-sociable and can manipulate people and use social skills to their advantage. Similarly the jock was just a person who was physically-minded first. I liked to think of it that, if a lightbulb wasn't working, the archetypes solutions would be:

JOCK – Smash it.
SOCIALITE – Convince someone else to fix it.
NERD – Find a YouTube tutorial and follow it to the second.
FOOL – Why do we even need lightbulbs? The moon is my lightbulb, man.

Reasons that I can find for only playing your own gender

Costume

Use it for the poster for sure, but don't let it pigeonhole you in the show.

Your cast are horrible at playing across gender

How? They're just playing people. How is it hard to play a woman if you're a man? You don't need to make your voice higher or swing your hips as you walk. Not all women fit that description. You can play close to yourself. Or play women you know, not stereotypes you have imagined or been exposed to. It's the same for playing people from cultures, ethnicities or sexualities other than your own. If you are playing a 'Chinese Person' in a scene, focus less on the 'Chinese' and more on the 'Person' part of that role. Think about how people from other cultures in your real life act, talk and behave. And if you don't know any, it's time to make some new chums.

Resetting gender

Since we're here, I'd also like to talk about 'resetting' gender in scenes. Like with names and a lot of other facts, it's tough to hold everything in our heads, but I do feel like the given gender of a character is often forgotten when it has been mentioned. I saw a scene yesterday where two men were playing men at a strip club and a third man was crawling along the floor seductively towards them. I was excited that they referred to the dancer as male. What a refreshing choice. He also seductively said his own name – 'Richard' – into the ear of one of the gents. The dancer character was referred to as male a couple more times. The game of the scene (it was a great scene) became that only the dancer could touch the men, but they could not touch him and they didn't see how that was different. At this point, the male dancer suddenly became female in everyone's speech. For me, it weakened the scene; not only because the reality was in flux but because what was an interesting comment on consent became a lot more clichéd.

I remember seeing a scene in Austin, Texas, where a lady was playing a priest. She hadn't defined her gender, but I assumed she was male in the context of the show so far and from the way she was playing. The first thing that happened with her (despite her setting up something else already) was that she was bullied by a group of male improvisers telling her that female priests weren't allowed.

In Barcelona I saw a show where a man initiated along the lines of: "All you sperm, get in here." Three men and two women entered as sperm and the two women were told to leave; that they were "not supposed" to be there. To add insult to injury, one of them was slapped on the ass as she left. I let out a weary sigh. If it had been a scene within a show where the women were playing outside of mothers and girlfriends, or if they'd been respected in general, perhaps that would have been a gentle meta-gag or societal commentary. What actually happened was that men were literally saying: "Male is ours, you women need to get out of this scene."

It happens a lot in beginners' classes. We had a game of freeze tag where a woman was playing a king and the man in the scene with her said: "Surely you mean queen?" We stopped and talked about the idea that anyone could play any character and if they asserted that they were a king, they were a king.

I'm not against a reframe but more often than not, a gender reframe is the result of poor listening and poor agreement, which breaks the reality and makes it a meta discussion about a role the woman has chosen to play.

A friend made an interesting point that women often choose to play traditional male roles on stage as male characters (like policemen, firemen, etc.) when we could be playing strong female characters in those roles. I think that's a super point.

Sometimes, I think male directors and male improvisers forget that they have been able to play most of the leading and empowered roles throughout their lives on stage. There is a special freedom for us female actors in being outside of the wife/mother/sex-worker roles we are commonly cast in.

Strategies

- If your director asks you only to play your own gender, question them. What is the artistic intention behind this? See if you agree with them or if they've even thought about why. Will you also be playing your own age?
- If you have asserted that you are playing a particular gender in a scene and someone resets that assertion, make your first choice clear again. I wouldn't normally suggest this (instead I would usually encourage you to find a justifiable compromise), but in this case I think it helps to keep pushing the point, even if it's on stage.
- If you are playing across gender, don't just play 'a man' or 'a woman', play someone you know of that gender.
- Don't put on a falsetto voice to play a woman.
- Don't keep adjusting your balls to play a man.
- Ask yourself if this high-status role could be a female character. Break the mould of playing historically male professionals as men: make that firefighter, doctor or award-winning microbiologist a woman.

How to Watch Improv

I'm at an improv festival and I'm watching four hours of improv a night. Sometimes I'm a horrible person and I'm just waiting until it's my show. Sometimes I'm spellbound. Sometimes I go into teacher or director head. So how should I watch an improv show? They're not necessarily my team and I might not know them, but I should still have their backs. Here are some tips for getting better at watching improv.

Support

When you are playing at a show, please watch the other acts. Yes, you may need to warm up; yes, you might be tired and you're on first, but think how much you appreciate it when the other groups stay to see you. If you are aware the other groups are very new or not so great, see it as your good deed for the day. If you've never heard of them, you should definitely watch them and see what they are up to. If you've seen them loads, great: stay and see what's happening with their show now; improv is different every time, right? Also, you don't have to awkwardly pretend in the pub that you did see them.

Don't just sit in the shadows at the back because you're a performer. There's no reason you should broadcast that by segregating yourself. Don't sit in the centre of the front row because that can be intimidating. You shouldn't be taking up paid punter seats, but you can make a theatre (or a pub room) look more full by filling up the empty seats once everyone else has arrived. Some nights don't always have enough staff to run the door smoothly (in London anyways) so if people need help finding seats, locating the bathroom or knowing if they have time to get a drink, try and help out. Once or twice at nights in London, technicians, front-of-house staff and the host haven't turned up. If you're comfortable filling a role at the last minute, you should do that. If the night is better, your show will be better.

See a broad spectrum of shows

Don't just watch the same group over and over again. It's all very well me watching *Baby Wants Candy* every day for several Edinburgh Festivals, but you need to see more than one thing. There are infinite ways of playing and there are a lot of shows and performers out there who can really inspire you. For a few years I thought that I'd seen all of shortform, then I took a punt on an American group in Edinburgh and had a really great night. They were slick, funny and I learned a lot of new games. Now I like shortform again. You might live nearer to one theatre or another or have trained at one school. Push yourself to go and see work in other schools and theatres. You never know: their style might be your new favourite.

Go and see your mates perform

I can't tell you how pleased I am when friends come to see my improv shows. I burned through all my favours in my first two years of stand-up, but sometimes muggle chums and improvisers will come to my shows. When I see them there I expect that they're playing and if they say, "Nah, I just fancied it", I glow. So give that feeling back. You love improv, remember? So go see your friends in their other shows, see how your fellow students are doing in their new team and be a nice person: a nice person who gets entertained and maybe has a lovely beer. When I watch my co-improvisers perform in other shows, I feel so lucky to play with them. Just last night I watched lots of The Maydays perform in other shows at the BIG IF (Barcelona Improv Festival) and I was so thrilled with how excellent they were. What a treat to get to play with those people, I thought. We can take our team buddies for granted but they're probably awesome and we're lucky to have them.

Don't sit there looking like an asshole

If you don't like a show, you really don't need to broadcast the fact. It doesn't help anyone, least of all you. You will come across as arrogant or mean or judgy. You don't have to pretend to laugh or give a standing ovation just to 'yes-and' the crowd, but it doesn't help the act for you to sit there with your arms crossed, looking moody. At least look open and encouraging. I've been in shows where I've caught the eye of a person who looks like they hate it and it's made me feel bad. That might even be in a sea of smiles and laughs. I've also seen fellow teachers in the audience do 'edit' gestures, wince when a performer denies something, point out a reality error like: "She was a tree, not a human, right?" (That last one was me being an asshole.) You're not really checking, you're showing off that you spotted what they missed.

Remember that the audience gets one hundred per cent of the information that is happening on stage and sometimes performers only get fifty per cent because of where we're standing and looking. It's much easier to think of funny bits and clever plots from your comfortable seat in the crowd.

Have a cheeky workout

As I mentioned earlier, you can always get more reps in by watching improvisation. It's another gym trip for your brain. Ideally it would be such a great show that you can just sit there and enjoy the shit out of it without even thinking. Often, though, we can be exposed to a lot of mediocre work, or in a workshop where we are sitting and watching two-person scenes forever, but there are necessarily times when we have to sit and watch.

Make your watching active. In the audience, learn all the character names like you would on stage, look for when you might edit, think about the themes, get ideas for 'follow-me' scenes or work out the subtext between the characters. Log where objects and scenery are placed, think of how you'd wrap up the story. I'm not saying you should be this in-your-head when you're playing on stage, but it's a great way of practising when you're the audience in class or you're watching a show.

Decide what you love

It was the worst show you've ever seen. But what did you love about it? There must have been something? One of the initiations was amazing, that guy was great at object work, the pianist was really good. It's a given that we dislike improv where people listen poorly to one another and treat each other badly, so let's get over that and find things we love. Also – did other people like it? Just because you didn't, that doesn't mean it's shit.

Pick something you can use

A person, a form, a style, an edit; anything you like. Here are some things that inspired me from the shows I watched last night:

- A form where we heard the backstage thoughts of the improvisers.

- Alternating a pianist underscoring scenes and having an existing song come through the PA.
- Monologuing to the audience as if they were one person.

As London veteran improviser Ruth Bratt pointed out to me, it's a great idea to ask the act whether they'd mind before you use something they created.

Only offer advice if you're asked

I've had people come up to me immediately after a show and give me notes. Not my director, not a teacher, sometimes a friend (who doesn't do improv) and sometimes a student of mine. It's weird, guys. First of all, I don't want my tiny little high ruined by this person being objective (and objectively negative) about the performance I've just given. I'm a pretty destructive critic of myself, so I really don't need a third person adding to the poo-poo party.

If you are asked for advice, check if that's really what they want; do they just need an ego boost or is this really a demand for creative notes? If they want notes, make them general things they can apply to their next show, not things they should have done this time. Also, you're not obliged to offer free advice.

Take action for your show

So we've learned how not to be negative about everything. But was there something in the show that annoyed you because it's something you're trying to work on yourself? I think it bugs me when people do a lot of love stories and awkward rom-coms and play ditzy American characters because *I* do too much of that. I'm just retroactively watching myself and saying "Enough!" So rather than deciding you don't like that show, see if there's anything you can change about your work or the group you work with.

Applaud

Ownership

Ownership is a really odd question in improvisation. Because we do something once and then throw it away, it seems strange that the question of ownership should come up. But who owns the exercises we do in classes and rehearsals and if you have performed something you'll never do again, why can't someone else write it down and use it?

Castings

I go to castings mainly for commercials. Because I'm an improviser, they'll normally have me making up dialogue on the spot within a given scenario. When I went to do some filming for an advert, we improvised for about thirteen hours and right at the end we were given a few sheets of one-liners that served as other choices for the final edit. Many of the lines on my sheet were ones that I had improvised at the audition and the recall, but where did the others come from? I had a sense of pride that mine were there, but afterwards I wondered if lines were being used from the jobs I didn't get. I am aware that a comedian recently asked for money when one of her improvised lines came up on a commercial, but that was a one-off. Know that even though your work is thrown into the world in the moment, it still has a lot of value and really, it belongs to you unless you've already sold it.

Live shows

There were rumours that a big American TV show had its writers go and watch improv (and even sketch shows) and then write up the best scenes with their own names attached. It's not something we worry about in the UK because our improv scene is still relatively small, but it might be worth filming your shows if you think that might be a concern. Also – write it up yourself and get the work! Make sure you credit your co-creators from an improvised stage show.

Formats

This is one of the trickiest ones for me. I have certainly used a lot of formats that I saw at iO Chicago and elsewhere. The Maydays had permission to do a version of *Whirled News Tonight*, but classic formats such as the Armando and the Harold are seen as freeware all over the world. When I have been taught a format in a class, I would find it weird not to go ahead and use or perform it. Why would you teach something you didn't want to be used on stage?

Then there's copying a form that you saw on stage and it's a very grey area. As mentioned previously, my husband and I do a podcast called *Destination Live* and there have been a number of occasions where people have asked (which was nice) if they could do a version. I said no. We created the format and it's the signature of the show. It's clearly copy-able to everyone who listens to it, as it's the same every week and on stage. Yet, we have some ownership of it.

The thing is, there are lots of formats out there that we can use as training tools and it's also easy to create and find new formats. I was teaching a group recently who invented a format that I had learned from a teacher they'd never met. They definitely hadn't come across it on stage before or learned from the people who taught it. There are just some forms that come naturally and might arrive in the zeitgeist at the same time.

Games and things you learned in class

In my classes – and indeed in this book – there are loads of exercises made by improvisers for improvisers, to improve their work. There are also a lot of people (like me – hello) whose income or part of their income derives from teaching improv. To whom do the exercises belong? In my classes I want to pass on these amazing techniques and exercises, but I always try and credit the teacher. I think that way, if those students learn the origin of the exercise, they may gravitate to a particular school or teacher. I buy clothes from charity shops and it just so happens that Zara, Warehouse and Louche (Joy) tend to be labels that I buy. I don't look at where they're from before I try them on, I guess they are just styles and fits that suit me; likewise with longform. Everything I heard about slow-burn and subtext led back to TJ and Dave, so I made a point of learning from them a few times. If you are a teacher or even a student, know the origin of the things you learned and if you pass it on, give credit where you can. It's hard to remember sometimes and I'm sure I've misremembered exercises and origins myself. Joe Samuel and I created lots of original improv exercises for *Truth in Song*, which is our workshop inspired by the styles of songwriters Sondheim and Jason Robert Brown. We are happy for those exercises to go out into the world, but equally, we would find it weird if someone else taught the same class without giving credit to the creators.

The biggest and best lesson would be to create your own work. Find something that no one else is doing. Existing forms are excellent training and – depending on the scene you're part of – a good way of getting audiences in. I urge you to be creative and find new ways of improvising that suit your own personality and your group.

Let's be kind and community-focused and give credit where we can.

Exciting! You've made it to the end of Week Ten.
Let's go through our weekly practice checklist.

Read

Did you read the chapter? Excellent!

Improvise

Exercises

Congratulate friends.

Action your jealousies.

Ask to be involved.

Watch friends.

Thank influences.

Play women who matter if you're female.

Play women you know if you're male.

Play genderless objects and people.

Watch

Did you manage to see a show?

What was it?

Reflect

Write down your notes or thoughts on what you read, saw or did this week.

Week Eleven:
The Real World

This week we'll be looking at the practical real-world applications of improvisation. How can you turn your excellent material into reusable scripted work? How drunk can you get on stage without messing everything up? Do you take your show for granted? How can you do the best possible casting to get into a new show?

Improv and Alcohol

Earlier this year, a friend asked me where my blog on alcohol and improv was. I hadn't yet written one. He felt like it was an essential question to cover as some of his troupe were "boozing before shows" and "coming to rehearsal with a four-pack". Here are my thoughts on drinking and improv.

Personally, I don't drink before I improvise, but unlike me, the majority of people aren't improvising as a career choice. For me, every show I play is a showcase (often to students) and can lead to teaching, coaching, directing or corporate sessions. I want to do my best work every time. I need my brain and a drink will take my skill level down. It might lower my inhibitions, but I'm in a place where I'm confident enough on stage that my inhibitions are pretty darn low anyways. Some people drink to help with the nerves. The thing is, if you always drink to deal with your nerves, your sober nerves aren't going to get any better, you're just going to build a dependency for drinking alcohol before every show. That might even increase over time when the gigs get bigger and scarier. Also, if you get rid of the nerves before a gig, you are probably putting a dampener on the high you would get afterwards.

For the majority of improvisers, improv is one of their chosen activities for downtime with friends in a culture where alcohol (in Britain anyways) is traditionally part of our relaxation. I'll have a few beers when I'm playing board games or D&D (nerd), so I can see why it seems to fit with a night of rehearsals or a low-pressure show. However, neither myself nor my friends care whether I'm good at board games and no one is paying to watch me play.

You're an adult (probably), so you can make your own decisions, but know that your choices around alcohol will affect the people you play with on stage and your relationships with them offstage. If you're slower and less physically aware, you make the other players work harder to support you and it stops being an even ensemble. If you're a solo improviser, I guess it's truly your decision. The audience is the other player for you. As a group player, there's also the simple fact that it's gross playing with someone who reeks of booze.

I confess that there are a couple of occasions where I do drink before (and sometimes during) improv. The first is New Year's Eve. For the last few years, I've joined the Hoopla NYE party at The Miller in London Bridge. Lots of improvisers get really drunk and do a bunch of shows. It is ticketed for the public, but mostly nerdy improvisers go (and a few long-suffering partners). Because everyone is drunk, most of the improv is pretty self-indulgent. I find that when I'm plastered, the first thing to go is my spatial awareness; I crash into people when I'm editing or edited and I miss a lot of offers that aren't happening directly in front of me. I slur, so that means any verbal offers I make are hard for other people to understand. I believe at the time that I'm the funniest person in the room, even though I can't hang onto a character or stop clowning around and breaking the believability of the scene. Once in a while and to an in-crowd, I think self-indulgent nonsense is pretty fun, especially when everyone is so pissed that we're all in the same boat.

The other instance in which I drink is the Living Room format. I do it because it was taught to me as a bunch of mates on their sofa drinking beers, jumping up and doing improv whenever they are inspired. Beers are for me a part of the form. It might lead us to play around a little more casually, to pretend like we are literally at home and enjoying one another honestly as we would do offstage. Even though I'm drinking beer, I don't drink before the show and the Corona that I'll take on with me won't really hit until towards the end. So really, I'm cheating. I'm having beer as a prop and it won't hamper what I'm saying or doing. Hopefully it makes our guests relax and know that it's a casual (often late-night) show.

There are other formats where drinking is a part of the entertainment factor of the show. Where one character is drinking throughout and the others are taking care of them, or there are 'live' drinks on stage for a genre show, or there are challenges or bits where alcohol is built into the show. I'm fine with those as long as it's mutually agreed and the audience knows that that is part of the gig. If someone is paying to see improv, they want to see the best show they can. If alcohol adds to the gimmick of the show and all of the performers are in agreement and enjoy that: cool.

There are veteran improvisers that I've seen drink a lot before a show and maybe even get plastered all the way through a thirty to fifty-hour Improvathon and it doesn't seem to make them bad improvisers (though I imagine they'd be better if they weren't hammered). Also, how the hell do they get through an Improvathon drunk? I would be asleep by hour four if I drank beer in a thirty-four-hour show.

There is no one I work with regularly that gets drunk before performing improv. I have a couple of chums who'll have a pint before they go on stage and I'm okay with that. I suggest that a sensible limit is the same as it is for driving. If you can drive a car, you can probably drive yourself and others through an improv show. In jam nights, I would apply the driving-limit rules and make that clear to potential performers. People new to improv can be a bit of a liability in terms of boundaries and trust anyway. If it's a fun night out and we live in a drinking culture, it's hard to ask people to be totally sober in an unpaid show.

If you really want a couple of drinks before a show or rehearsal, check in with your group first. If it worries anyone that people are drinking beforehand, come to a reasonable compromise so that everyone is happy. As for other drugs, I think the above is probably true for those too. Experiment with anything you want if it's part of the agreed show (depending where you stand on the legality and safety of that substance) and don't give your fellow improvisers a bunch of work because you're selfishly indulging.

There are also lots of members of our improv community who don't drink and have no interest in doing so. Remember to respect their choices and don't give them a bunch more work on stage!

All this talk of beer makes me want a beer.

I'm off to get a beer.

Repurposing Improv

If you perform an amazing piece of improv, there's no reason why you shouldn't make it into a scripted piece. Hone it, try it in front of audiences and see if it still stands up. Writing itself is very much like improvising; it's improvising on paper. The only difference is looking back over it and editing it. Also, you're more likely to be writing alone than in a team.

I worked on sketch satire shows for a few years: *The Treason Show* in Brighton and London's longest-running sketch comedy *NewsRevue*. I've also made theatre shows (including a solo show) and a comedy musical, all of which used improvisation as a large part of the creative process and all in slightly different ways.

With writing, you can use the ideas (and jokes) that annoyingly come to you after an improv scene. If you improvise a scene, the audience has joy and forgiveness for what you are doing. The audience often gets the joke at the same time as the improviser. If the audience knows it's pre-written, they are expecting more.

Simply re-hashing improv would be like trying to relive a funny conversation you had in the pub; "you had to be there". That's what improv is: "you had to be there" because there, it's really funny. The tip for written work is that it always needs to come across as fresh, you have to be enjoying it and finding it as funny as you did the first time you did it. My dad's a children's author and one of his best tips to me as a child was always to remember how you felt about an idea the first time it came to you. If a joke made you laugh, if a plot made you excited, if a character made you empathise, that's how it's going to come across the first time someone else hears it.

I directed a theatre show called *The Watery Journey of Nereus Pike* starring Laura Mugridge. She wanted to make a solo show about the sea and about a man with a big white beard. That's all we had to start with, so we danced, talked, explored his environment (which was a lighthouse and also the depths of the Mariana Trench) and played with imagined scenarios. The things that we found fun, we worked up into a fantastic piece of theatre.

There are lots of ways of doing this. The ones I've used the most are:

Keep improvising it

You can do this in front of an audience like Second City does. Michael Gellman suggests doing it four times for your group, going away and discussing what you liked that the other person did and coming back to do it three more times. At that point, you'll start discovering what it's really about and the bits that stick are the best bits. The next step is to put it up in front of an audience and keep using the feedback of laughter to improve the sketch and to trim the fat from the dialogue.

Write it down and rehearse it

You can record improv shows and literally transcribe how they went. Take that transcription as your first draft and stand it up in a rehearsal room with your director. Change lines, reorder it and add bits as you go, but you have a solid backbone for it that started live on stage.

Keep it fresh

Our *Ghostbusters* musical fan-tribute show in Edinburgh was like a lot of comedy shows: there would be ad-libs in some of the performances that got a great response. We'd try them for a couple more days and if they were still received well, we'd add them to our script. At the end of our run we edited the script adding in all the pieces that had grown and developed over twenty-six shows. That meant that when we came back to it a year later it was much richer. We found that too many ad-libs would ruin the flow of the scripted material, so small changes would come in here and there over time.

Collect

Shenoah Allen of the acclaimed US comedy duo Pajama Men shared his techniques in a recent workshop. We stepped out of improvised scenarios every time we enjoyed a line and wrote it down, then we went right back into the scene. We'd build up a batch of these scene ideas, jokes, lines of dialogue and character ideas to use later. We also worked with pre-planned characters in improvised scenarios to find out more about them. How do they react in this or that scenario or with this other character we have made? In order to build a show, then, Shenoah and Mark (Chavez) would spend six weeks or more finding a loose narrative to have these characters, ideas and dialogue play out in an hour-long devised work.

I was in a comedy show at the Edinburgh Festival this year called *Knightmare Live*. It was a stage show based on the British TV series *Knightmare* and it had a loose structure that the cast created through devising. There was a lot of interaction with the public and two comedians on the panel each day. The panel were there for one night only, so any bits you had planned may or may not come out in the show. It was a little bit of script, a little bit of improv and a Choose Your Own Adventure kind of storyline. Paul, the director, had to remind me to keep the bits that worked. I would be improvising new stuff every single day when a tried and tested joke was better and there was still tons of room for making stuff up. Oddly, delivering the same goods night after night was scarier to me than making everything up.

Your scripted show can continue to be worked on when it's up in front of an audience. It's very rare that say, an Edinburgh show will remain unchanged from the first to the last show. If one bit doesn't ever work in front of an audience, that's a bit you'll need to cut, improve or replace. If one piece works really well on its own, but doesn't work in the fullness of the show, you'll have to take it out or use it in another show. Cutting it is one of the hardest things to do.

Don't Take Improv for Granted

My husband and I get married every year and a day. It's called a handfasting and it helps us not to take one another for granted. We have had eight handfastings at the time of writing; every year and a day since the first one.

Perhaps take a moment to look at the teams you play with, the classes you take and your personal development every so often. How can you and your team get better? Are you still excited to be working with them every year?

It's easy to take improv for granted. I was talking with another London improviser recently about how some teams settle into their regular show without pushing themselves. It's not unusual for an established team to get sloppy or self-referential. Rather than getting complacent, keep learning from every corner of the world. That doesn't just mean improv classes, it means training in other fields of theatre and physical disciplines and just plain life-living. When I travel outside the UK, my improv improves (even if I just go on holiday). I'm a more rounded person with more life experience when I've done something outside of my routine. The more you experience life, the more range your work will have.

Keep watching shows and be aware of the next generation of improvisers that comes along. They may have completely different ways of doing things and you should experiment with new ideas so that you don't get staid. I was lucky enough to play with several veterans last month. They all had around twenty to thirty years of experience in improvisation – much more than me – but one was completely confounded by longform. I wondered how you make a career in improvisation without noticing longform. She was excellent as a character player, but resistant to editing (apart from the host announcing the next scene). Try to play in any way and try out new tools without fear of failure (not because you can't fail, but because that's how we learn and also how comedy is made).

The Maydays take research and development very seriously. We make sure that at least once a year we do a week of full-time training as a team. In 2016, for example, we all travelled to Chicago and handpicked some of our favourite players and teachers to coach us. We learned from Jorin Garguilo, Rich & Rebecca Sohn, Mick Napier, Adal Rifai, Farrell Walsh, Bill Arnett (our spirit animal) and TJ Jagodowski. I appreciate that's not an option for everyone, but a minimum requirement is to rehearse regularly. You might be on a lot of teams and lack the time to rehearse with each one of them. You will find that the shows you just drop into stagnate, or that everyone is working harder to help you adapt to the show.

The thing that I see most in successful improvisers is that they not only keep doing it regularly, but they keep learning. You don't have to be a genius or super-funny, but you have to be able to break and rebuild your habits sometimes. The other thing that keeps groups solid, is their personal commitment to one another. Take the time to see those people outside of improv.

Exercise

Make a commitment to your improv. Choose to do at least one of the following over the next six months. Book it and put it in your diary.

- Take a class that complements improv (like Meisner, mask, dance or singing).
- Take an improv class that is different to ones you've done before.
- Make a date with your improv group to do something other than improv (go bowling, go to a museum, go walking, play a game together online).

Don't let money be a limiting factor for these things. Going for a walk won't cost anything and watching exercises online then trying them out with your group can be an alternative to paying for a class.

Twelve Tips on Casting for Improv Shows

I've been asked a handful of times over the last week if I have advice for how to do well in improv castings. I coach, teach and direct improv shows and I'm also an actor, so I know the stresses that can come with auditions. I can't speak for everyone, but I can tell you what I would be looking for in an improv audition.

1. Do your research

Who are these guys? What is their style? Where do they play? What do you like about them? Get ready to answer questions about why you want to be in this group. Also, check in with yourself; is this where you want to be?

2. Dress appropriately

Make sure you're wearing something you can move in and something that won't show off your bits when you do physical work. Scrappy clothes indicate that you don't care or that you're poor because you've *never* got a job *ever* (and even if that's the case, you don't want them to know that).

3. It starts on the way

You never know who you will bump into on your way to the casting, so be in 'polite and lovely' mode the whole time. Make a point of saying hello to the other people at the venue and in the waiting room. You want them all to be your allies and it might be the only connection you get with your fellow players before you're put in a scene with them.

4. Be on time

Duh! Leave lots of time for disasters en route. Be early. Get a cuppa and walk around the block. Being late is the stupidest reason for not getting a job. Even if it's the only time you've ever been late, they will think you're generally a late or unreliable person. If you *do* have a series of disasters that makes you late, try to take a breath before you go in. Don't be flustered, just apologise and join in with a minimum of fuss.

5. Bring water

Some people don't. Amazing.

6. Support, not showboating

Your instinct will be that you want to be seen, to stand out, but if you have a good improviser running the casting, they will notice how good or bad you are at support. Even in auditions, it's important to make the other person look good by really listening to them, building on their ideas and editing at a time that serves the scene. How many people are playing? Work out the percentage you should show up on stage. Don't hang back or be in every scene. You don't need to do every single idea you have, but serve the scene or the set you are performing in.

7. Be a great audience

If you are watching other people at any point in the casting, there is nothing nicer than laughing and smiling and caring about the other improv that's happening. It may feel counter-intuitive because *you* want to get the job, but you'll look like a nice human that enjoys improv and who doesn't want that person on their team?

8. Show your range

Just like a good show, you're going to need variation in your performance. If you're initiating a lot, make sure you do some scenes where you're responding and reacting off someone else's initiation. If you've played a lot of big, cartoonish characters thus far, play some real-world characters that are close to you, play honest and truthful over funny. Do talky scenes after doing a lot of quiet or physical scenes and so forth.

9. Be yourself

If you're very adaptable and you can blag your way into a show without it really suiting you and how you like to play, that's not going to be much fun. Make sure that you make choices because they're exciting to you, not because you're trying to prove anything. If you get it, they will be casting you for you and you'll have a much nicer time. I have found that being myself has got me a lot more work that trying to guess what a casting director wants and trying to please them.

However...

10. Take direction

Listen out for what you are being asked to do. It sounds simple, but *so* many people just can't take direction. If your director wants you to play in a different way, or try something out, go with it; it's one less decision you have to make! The director really wants you to be the best. They are not looking for anyone to fail. The best outcome for them is that everyone is brilliant.

11. Be kind to yourself if you don't get it

There are three main reasons for not getting a job:

- You aren't good enough… yet.
- You are good enough, but you were too nervous and it threw you off your game.
- You are totally good enough, you're just not a 'fit' with that group.

The solutions are:

- Get better at improv – but we all want that anyway, right?
- Hey – you'll be less nervous every time. This one is prepping you for another one in the future. I tell myself that castings are a 'free workshop' (because they are) and that stops me being nervous.
- They may even love you and your work, but already have someone who has similar superpowers to you. That's cool. They may need you in future. Or you could have knocked it out of the park, but they didn't like it. So you probably wouldn't have a great time working as a team anyhow. Never mind.

12. Above and beyond

You are much more likely to be liked and noticed if the group have seen you at their shows. It indicates that you really enjoy what they do. Go say hi, but don't hang around them awkwardly! See if you can help on lights or sound or selling tickets. If going to their shows feels like a chore, it's probably not a group you want to become a part of.

My favourite advice (I think I learned this from a Bryan Cranston video).

"Auditioning is the whole of the job. You came and you did your best. It's just a bonus if you actually book the work. Think of it that way and you'll be satisfied before you even know the result."

Bonne chance!

Shit, son! You've made it to the end of Week Eleven.
Let's go through our weekly practice checklist.

Read

Did you read the chapter? Hope so!

Improvise

Repurposing improv exercises

- Choose a setting for your scene, like a lighthouse. Have one person walk through the environment and talk about the things that they see, presenting them to the audience.

  > "This is a cozy bedroom with floral covers on a double bed. There is a softly glowing nightlight plugged in by the door. There is a book on reptiles sat on a table by the bed…"

  Now tell a story about why those things were there. Who chose the floral covers and what sort of person are they? Why have a nightlight? Is someone scared of the dark or do they need to get up a lot in the night? Is someone a fan of reptiles or was this book a present that needs to be on show?

  As we worked on *The Watery Journey of Nereus Pike*, we wove each of the objects in our lighthouse into other parts of our narrative, or we created objects from the narrative to be placed in the lighthouse. Nothing was wasted.

- Try Michael Gelman's Second City technique of re-improvising one scene. We tried this in The Maydays and it was amazing seeing how the seventh version was so much richer than the first, even though the ones in the middle dipped.

- Try filming some scenes, pick your favourite, type it out and work on it like a play. Be brutal with your editing and don't be afraid of changing the order of events, cutting lines or losing and gaining characters.

There are a lot of resources out there for writing sketch comedy and devising theatre – and if you're an improviser, you already have a really valuable and relevant skill.

Watch

Did you manage to see a show?

What was it?

Reflect

Write down your notes or thoughts on what you read, saw or did this week.

Week Twelve:
Inspiration

It's the final week of your journey and you have done incredibly well to get this far. Congratulations on your dedication and for putting the time aside to be a better improviser.

This week we'll be looking at some larger themes; sorting your shit out, strategies for improv that you can keep coming back to, and little bits of inspiration that I always revisit when I need it.

Get Your Shit Together

…Or get your shit as together as possible. If you are unfit, unhappy or disorganised there are a lot of things you can do to help yourself and a lot of people out there who can help you if you ask.

Apply 'yes-and' to other parts of your life.

Your body

Everybody's body is different, so let's all try and get as close as we can to a good state of fitness.

> "I am a mime, my body is my tool."
> Rowan Atkinson's character in *Not the Nine O'Clock News*

Keep your body in the best condition you can. I'm really not a big fan of exercise and it takes a huge amount of effort for me to do it. When I do, of course, I feel amazing and the cumulative effect of regular exercise means that I am more physically engaged and choose to use my body more on stage. If you're brand new to exercising, I'd recommend doing one of these or similar:

- Seven (Guess what? It's a seven-minute workout app).
- A 'Couch to 5K' training programme (I used the NHS podcast).
- Zombies, Run! (A story-based running app).

None of these cost money to try and all you need is a chair for the first one and some running shoes for the second and third ones. They have all the guidance you need to complete the activities and after the first couple of weeks, it can feel pretty good. Running isn't an option for everyone, of course, but there are a lot of ways for everyone to stay connected to and aware of their physicality.

Last year I was at the Edinburgh Festival Fringe doing two shows a day. I spent £60 on a spa membership for the month. I went to the steam room and the pool almost every day. It was the first time I managed to keep my voice for the whole month despite improvising a musical and doing a lot of silly voices in *Knightmare Live* every day. My energy levels were great. I managed to dodge the flu and exhaustion that everyone around me was suffering from. Eat well and keep moderately fit. We all know that's what we need to do and yet we make so many excuses.

If you don't have the personal willpower to do exercise at home or in your local park, get a personal trainer or do it with a friend. I don't like the gym. You might, but it's not your only option. I taught pole-dancing and hula-hooping for years, which didn't feel like exercise at all because they were fun. Find the right thing for your budget, your willpower, your body and your schedule – and stick to it.

Your brain

There are a lot of improvisers in the world who live with anxiety and depression in many different forms. I am not an expert in either, but I've had periods of my life where I've felt depressed and anxious. I learned some great tools from cognitive behavioural therapy (CBT), neuro-linguistic programming (NLP) and hypnosis. I'd recommend *How to Lift Depression Fast: The Human Givens Approach* by Joe Griffin and Ivan Tyrrell. I personally found it useful and often send it to friends who are having a tough time. I'm not suggesting you can sort out all your issues by reading a book, but it is important to look at the issues we have, even if that means finding day-to-day coping strategies.

Look at your diet too; food and booze hugely affect your mood. Try meditating. The Headspace app gives you ten ten-minute mediations for free which are very calming and introduce you to the idea of mindfulness.

Your environment

A tidy house means a tidy mind. I really believe that. Get rid of junk, have a nice place to work or relax and enjoy where you live and where you work. Look into feng shui. Read *The Life-Changing Art of Tidying* by Marie Kondo, enjoy how bonkers she is and then actually apply the stuff she recommends. Get ready to store all your clothing vertically and have a wardrobe full of clothes that slope up to the right...

You will take photographs of your underwear drawer.

Your work practice

Don't find excuses not to do things. Get the hell on with it. I recommend reading *The War of Art* by Stephen Pressfield. On a purely practical get-it-done, organise-your-admin level, read *How to Be a Productivity Ninja* by Graham Allcott.

Be on time

Mostly I've always been one of those people that will turn up really early. I often leave too much time and end up walking around the block for twenty minutes until it's acceptable to be there. Perhaps because I commute on public transport, I leave this window of 'fuck-up' time. However, I got pretty annoyed that although I would go out of my way to make sure I was somewhere on time, others wouldn't have the same courtesy and I'd end up not only being twenty minutes early, but then waiting another twenty minutes for other people to turn up and therefore wasting a good amount of my day. Lately, I've started to slip. Now, unless I have something very important (like a casting or a show) to go to, I leave much less fuck-up time. Doing this, though, I start to get why people run late. You just look at one more email, then you don't leave enough time to put make-up on or have a shower so you rush through that and then you're tired and stressed so you stop for a coffee and you're another five minutes late.

It's simple: just be on time. Don't be crazy-woman early and don't be late. When I teach, I start teaching right on time (unless it's a one-off class). That way, I reward the people who are on time with a fun warm-up (even if it's a two-person warm-up) and the latecomers have a positive reason to make it on time the next week. There are always students who finish work late and have transport issues, etc., but for the most part, this drills timing into them and we all get more time on the stage without resenting one another.

I have my own opinion, of course, but I'd rather work with someone who is really good and punctual than someone slightly better but always late.

Vertical Strategies

Think of this section as the improv version of Brian Eno's *Oblique Strategies*, except they're more like Vertical Strategies because they're straight up. You can read them all – sure – but why not just dip in next time you have a show or rehearsal and put your finger on one. Choose that to be your focus for the day or the week. We have the rest of our lives, we don't have to nail every single thing every time. When we get improv 'right' we can just quit.

> ### 'Good' is as good as 'bad' in a workshop.

Kevin McDonald (Kids in the Hall)

It was an offhand remark, but one that really resonated with me. If the people just before you in a workshop totally nailed a scene, it's nice to know that there is no pressure for you to do the same. You are learning, the more you fuck it up, the more you get to learn.

> ### I hear you do a great impression of...

Shannon O'Neill (UCB)

Shannon introduced a game where you stand in a circle and one person announces "[Name of person in circle], I hear you do a great impression of [famous person/animal] doing [a task]." That person then performs the impression to the best of their ability.

273

The lovely thing is that you likely cannot deliver on this impression, so the pressure drops away and you just commit as hard as you can.

You can afford to tell the truth: no one will believe you.

Del Close, but brought to my attention by my absolute heroes TJ and Dave

It's sometimes much easier to start with what you genuinely think and believe and it's safe being confessional because you are in a fictional environment. I told an absolutely true (and secret) story in a recent show that my husband jovially berated me for afterwards. I pointed out that no one would ever know it was true and we smiled to ourselves.

Lose.

Tom Salinsky (Spontaneity Shop)

This was really a personal note that I now find myself giving to other people who need it. Tom was coaching me and Chris Mead for Project2 and I found that I was trying so hard to nail every exercise that I was forgetting to let my characters fail. Failing as a character is not failing as an improviser. I don't need to be in control, I don't need to know what's happening and losing is often the funniest, strongest position to take in a scene.

> **If you know the genre, you know the climax.**

Anthony Atamanuik (UCB)

I was learning The Movie with Anthony, and this advice was a bit of a revelation. Freeform longform is my favourite; it really makes me happy, but I do play in (and direct) genre improv, so to know that the climax is already there was a great mind-change for me. Without playing any preceding scenes, we jumped straight to the climax of any given genre. They were perfect, that *is* what would happen. Only the specifics change.

> **The emotional connection is more important than the facts. If the emotional connection changes, it's like walking through an object-work table.**

TJ Jagodowski and Dave Pasquesi (iO Chicago)

You know that moment in improv when someone spends a while establishing (wiping down, putting a drink on, scratching their name into) a table and then another improviser walks straight through it? Unless it's justified as a ghost, a hologram or whatever, the audience is left unsettled. In this class, we worked hard on recognising emotional connection and I see that it is just the same. If we as an audience felt like there was underlying sexual attraction at the beginning of a scene and it disappears – unexplained – by the end, the scene seems like a total lie.

What's the 'about' about?

Kevin McDonald (Kids in the Hall)

This was a sketch-writing workshop using improvisation, but this question is equally applicable to pure improv. Sure, Spinal Tap may be about a band on tour, but the 'about' about is the friendship between two characters and how it falls apart. What are the larger themes at play in your improv?

Everything you need is already here.

TJ Jagodowski

I lost count of the number of times TJ would stop the scene within a few seconds because we were denying our own offers. Look at how you're standing. What was that expression about? Did you feel that underlying tension? You seem like colleagues, no? Let's just take a second to acknowledge every micro-offer, then we hardly need to work at all.

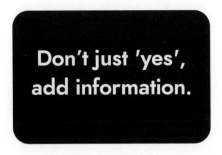

**Don't just 'yes',
add information.**

Adal Rifai

We've been learning 'yes, and' since Day One, but actually we can be a lot more efficient. Once we get the first line, we can really go to town on detail. Take a moment to check if you are 'and'-ing, or if you're just 'yes'-ing with a lot of words.

**Fuck,
marry, kill.**

Rich Sohn

Using these basic human extremes of emotion, we played out (sometimes the same) scenes, pushing in each direction. Marry is broadly 'negotiate' and the others are exactly what you think they are. Really, everything boils down to this.

**Find
an emotional
point of view.**

Farrell Walsh

When you get a one-word suggestion, there are lots of ways to take it into a scene. Think about how you attach to 'strawberry' as a word; does it make you feel summery, fruity, allergic? Attach to the context of the word; how are you at a tennis match? Bored, exhilarated, lost? Is there anywhere else you'd feel that feeling? Perhaps you'd also feel lost at a supermarket like you did when you were small. Boom; there's a feeling and a setting for your scene.

Here are some of mine.

Show up.

After a few years, it seems like the easiest thing to do in improv: get the hell on stage, but I found myself hesitating in my first Chicago show because I was playing in a thirteen-strong cast with veteran players. Hesitating doesn't help anyone. Show the hell up, that's the only way you can follow through on supporting your fellow improvisers. We're always being told to make our fellow players look good, to serve the show; well, this is the best way of doing it. Get on stage. If you're auditioning your idea or anyone else's, you have already lost the battle and the moment for that idea will have passed.

Make room for others.

This is the other thing I learned from playing with the cool kids: there is always a hand reached out; we are in this together, no one will be left behind. Bring someone on who hasn't got on stage yet, leave space for them to respond and play. Treat them like a genius, artist and poet.

Stage time is everything.

It's all very well learning a lot of theory about improv and reading books and quoting the teachers you've had, but it's up to you to create your own philosophy and style. The only way to learn to be a successful performance improviser is to hit the stage regularly, watch a lot of shows and play with people that challenge you.

Incredible Women (Who Changed the Way I Improvise)

This is the second part of my Vertical Strategies, but it's in the form of a tribute to the women that have inspired me the most. There are many, but here are some that stand out.

Susan Messing

On asking friends what Susan was like as a teacher they would often attempt an impression of her, including catchphrases and a lot of swearing, which was a little intimidating. When I finally met her – in a workshop weekend in London – I found her to be utterly refreshing. She immediately cut through all of the bullshit: a truth-sayer who would challenge you hard and make you feel totally secure at the same time. She focused on the self and the team as completely symbiotic creatures in improv, which now seems obvious. I met her again in Nottingham where I was performing in Project2 and she was doing *Messing With a Friend*. We chatted in the pub and she invited me to play in *Messing With a Friend* in Chicago (which it took me two years to follow up on). It was incredible and she is one of the best scene partners I have ever had.

> Advice I use most from Susan Messing:
> "If you're not having fun, you're the asshole."

Rebecca Sohn

The Maydays invited Rich and Rebecca Sohn over from the Annoyance Theatre, Chicago. They immediately got to work on The Maydays and after a week of work, our shows were much stronger. Our intimacy and trust with one another as performers grew and we remembered to take it seriously, but also, not at all seriously. We took more risks and noticed more what the dynamic was on stage. Rebecca struck me as a strong and hilarious woman; seeing what she is up to in her comedy life is a constant and useful kick in the ass for me professionally.

Jill Bernard

Friends talked a lot about Jill and I was excited to do a class with her. I had heard that she was fun and playful. I booked on a solo improv workshop. I have and had no desire to do a solo improv show, but I coach a handful and I was working on a solo scripted piece. I was the asshole in the room and one of my first questions was: "How do you do solo improv and not come across as smug?" It was a genuine question as I think solo improv has a lot of fundamental flaws (ask me in the pub) and this is one of them. I had never seen Jill perform, so it wasn't about her work, just about solo improv in general. Her answer delighted me. Rather than practical solutions on how to counter looking like you were a smart git, she brightly said: "Why shouldn't you be smug, you're doing a *solo improv show!* That's amazing!"

Nancy Howland Walker

I met Nancy at Second City in 2005. Rachel Blackman and I were taking the intensive course there and saw that she was running a musical improv class at the weekends. There were three weekends and we had missed the first one. Nevertheless, Nancy was completely open-hearted and shoved us right in at the deep end with solos on the first day. I don't think I've ever been as scared but nor have I learned a tool that has been so life-changing and beautiful as improvising songs. Nancy is one of the warmest and most caring teachers I have ever had.

Favourite advice from Nancy Howland Walker on the way to sing Sondheim:
"Whatever the piano is doing, do something else."

Charna Halpern

Charna is many things to improv and known as the mother of longform, so I was very excited to spend a week with her in London in 2013. The first two days were tough and I didn't connect with her much at all, but after that it was like a detective novel; she had been watching and listening and working out who we all were as people. I don't think she cared what our improv was like until she knew who we were. At that point, she broke off from improv entirely, got us all to tell personal stories sitting on stage and connecting with one another. Immediately, of course, our improv skyrocketed. We dropped our bullshit of trying to impress her and one another and just played. That's the kind of teacher I want.

My favourite form from Charna Halpern (originally performed by The Family) was the Living Room (see Chapter Seven) where you tell stories on a sofa with a beer in your hand and whenever you're inspired you get up and do a scene.

Rachel Blackman

Rachel is my twoprov partner of eleven or more years. We played in The Maydays together for a lot of that time too. Rachel is an incredible friend and a ridiculously talented actress and theatre-maker. While I'm off being silly, she makes a practice of her art. She knows how to do the work, how to be professional and how to make improv that matters. She is the one who encouraged me to train in Chicago, because if you're going to learn, learn from the best. We don't get to do our show as often as we would like, but when we do (even if months have gone by) it is still the show that I am the most proud of. It's theatre, actual theatre. It's funny and it's often ridiculous, but I've tried to bottle the connection I have with Rachel in other teams and it's just not possible. She is the TJ to my Dave (or the other way around).

I hope you get the chance to work with some or all of these bonkers geniuses. Every minute I've spent with them has made my work better and my heart a little warmer.

As well as trying out some of these nuggets of wisdom, start collecting your own. For every coach or teacher you have, make a note of at least one thing that changed the way you improvise, or at least something that made you perform or think differently for a moment. Perhaps it's something you've felt all along, but you've never heard anyone express before. Perhaps it's even something you hugely disagreed with them about! Jot down their name, the thing you learned and the exercise that goes with it. Add the context to help you remember how it felt and who you played with.

Here's some space for your own collected wisdom:

Date:

Teacher/Coach:

Wisdom

Context

Exercise

Date:

Teacher/Coach:

Wisdom

Context

Exercise

Date:

Teacher/Coach:

Wisdom

Context

Exercise

Date:

Teacher/Coach:

Wisdom

Context

Exercise

Date:

Teacher/Coach:

Wisdom

Context

Exercise

Ten Ways to Level Up

Perhaps you're new to improv and you can't wait to be more confident on stage. Perhaps you've been doing it for a year or two and it's still really fun, but you feel a bit stuck in improvising the same kind of thing. Perhaps you've been doing improv for five years or more and you're not getting into the shows you want or being asked to join groups. Perhaps you're a veteran; you teach and you play in a well-known team, but you want to excel. Here are a handful of ways that can really help you up your game. Some of them are pretty obvious, but putting them together will make you a superhero. Spandex, people. Spandex.

Here we go; in order of difficulty, easy to hard:

(I'm assuming you're already taking classes and probably doing shows. If you're not, start there.)

1. Watch

Oh my gods, it is crazy how many students I get that have never even seen improv. They might remember *Whose Line Is It Anyway?* from the '90s or they went to London's Comedy Store one time, but that ain't the same. If you really want to be good at comedy, you need to see what other people are doing, and regularly. It doesn't even matter if the shows you see are not very good, or if they're not the kind of style you're into. In fact, great! Now you know what you don't want to do on stage. That's just as awesome as knowing what you do want to do. That's why people go crazy for the Edinburgh Festival Fringe; it's where you'll see the best and worst shows of your life and you can be inspired and reassured by where you are on that scale.

2. Play with strangers

Jams are a really good way of cutting your teeth in improv. A jam has become parlance for a show where any audience members can get up and play, including total beginners. Playing with less experienced people makes you better at support and driving the scene. Playing with more experienced players gives you an ego boost and helps you to take risks and see what it can feel like to be truly supported. Both break you out of habits that you may have fallen into by playing with the same people. Jams aren't the only option for this. Pick some people you'd love to play with and ask them if they'd like to do a gig with you. Maybe put on a night where you do your show, they do their show and you all play in a mash-up at the end. What's the worst that could happen? They'll say no? Well, that's the same outcome as you not asking, so you might as well tip the odds.

3. Geek out

For the most part, improvisers are nerds (or at least improv nerds) so they like to talk about it in great detail. You can swap philosophies, understand people's intentions for their work and hear about new forms and exciting shows that are going on. You might even make a new bud. Aw.

4. Learn with a different school

Have you taken classes at an improv school? Great! Well done you for learning. Now it's important to remember that improv is not maths. There is no one way of doing it right, no matter what people tell you. You *will* get teachers that contradict one another because comedy is in the eye of the beholder. I say hooray for that! Superb! Try out another school. Learn a different way in. If you've been taught to always bring an idea or premise on to the stage, go somewhere where you are forced to be organic and build from nothing with your scene partner. If you've been at a very physical school, go somewhere where wordplay is the most coveted thing. That way we all get a thousand more tools to play with and we're not judgy about whose way is better. We can choose in the moment, or be appropriate to the show we're performing in. This totally goes for improv veterans too. If you are teaching and you haven't been to someone else's class in a year, you're probably stagnating. Book a visiting coach from the States, do a week of clowning, go learn Meisner. But please, you haven't 'finished' learning improv.

5. Do two-person improv

I can't recommend this enough. Doing a two-person show with Rachel Blackman after exclusively playing with The Maydays taught me *so much*. When there are just two of you on stage you have to take responsibility. You really need to tune in with that other person, really make their offers count, really listen, really commit and so forth. Basically every piece of improv guidance you've ever had is underlined and pushed. You'll find out much more clearly who you are as an improviser. Half of that show is you and all of it is both of you. Don't just stick to one partner: screw around, play with as many partners as will take you. Each one will magnify a style that you have in you and make you a better improviser.

6. Travel

I'm saying this partly because I took Project2 to Sweden recently and it reminded me how useful it is not only to watch shows, but to watch shows from other countries. Things (comedy, theatre, edits, framing, character types) we take for granted in our own countries are not necessarily the norm elsewhere. To generalise horribly, Brits and Americans are much less physical in their work than most Europeans. Also, it's really beneficial being outside of your home country when you're watching shows, because that different environment makes you more open to new things. Most people will also be leaving their work (and their loved ones) behind so it can be more immersive.

7. Read

It's pretty difficult to learn improv from a book but if you're taking classes or doing shows, it's a great way to supplement your learning. Some of my favourites are:

- Jill Bernard's *Small Cute Book of Improv*
- *Truth in Comedy: The Manual for Improvisation* by Charna Halpern, Del Close and Kim 'Howard' Johnson
- *Improvise: Scene from the Inside Out* by Mick Napier
- *Improvisation at the Speed of Life: The TJ and Dave Book*

8. Tape your shows

Okay, this one is a total nightmare and really just for those of you who really want to push your level up. I've done it for blocks of time in the past and this year I am taping most of my shows. It's a diagnostic tool and it's very useful as a leveller when you realise that bad shows weren't as bad as you imagined and good shows weren't as good as you thought. Be kind to yourself and your team if you do do diagnostics. The best way to approach it is not to criticise the specifics of that show, but to ask yourself what can you take from it for your next show. Make sure it's full of positives and not just what you think you fucked up. A positive note might be "We are really good at leaving space in dialogue, let's keep doing that" or a constructive note might be "Let's use the physical space more imaginatively next time." I'd steer you away from critiquing one another's improv and keep it about the show.

9. Teach

This one isn't for everyone, but leading a session or even a warm-up for your team can really help you be a better improviser. Breaking down what exercises are for, reading the energy in the room and setting goals for your scenework can be really insightful. Teaching and coaching teaches me so much that I spend a lot of my time doing it. There's always a balance, though. Make sure you perform if you teach and road-test everything you're telling other people to try.

10. Do something else

If you're in deep, this might be the most important one. Take time to do something – anything – else. For most people the other thing might be their day job, or another hobby, but for those of us that are doing it 24/7, it's really important to have outside influences. I like to read curated *Stack* magazines to get a different worldview, to watch films and scripted theatre, to hula-hoop or to play D&D and board games with friends. If you don't do anything else, where will your inspiration come from? Improv will be a little in-jokey if you aren't having other life experiences. Also, improv will seem a bit too important and you won't have as much fun. Remember, it's just make-'em-ups.

That's it. You've made it to the end of Week Twelve and the entire book! Well done!

Let's go through our weekly practice checklist one last time.

Read

Did you read the chapter? The last one!

Improvise

Exercise I love the most from Rebecca Sohn (Annoyance)

Touching noses and foreheads with your scene partner throughout a whole scene and not breaking eye contact.

Favourite Jill Bernard exercise

LOSERBALL: throw a mime ball around the circle. No one ever manages to catch it, and every miss is met with celebration.

Other exercises

Choose a Vertical Strategy at random and use it in your next rehearsal or show.

Make one simple action towards getting your shit together (like being on time more often or clearing out some house junk).

Watch

Did you manage to see a show?

What was it?

Reflect

Write down your final notes or thoughts on what you read, saw or did this week.

Epilogue

I hope you enjoyed this longform workbook and congratulations on finishing it. Like any worthwhile relationship, you will find that your love of improvisation changes over time. You may feel like you fall out of love with it occasionally, but your commitment and excitement for it will return at a deeper level each time. Seek the inspiration you need by watching and playing. Connect with your friends and family both inside and outside of the art form and enrich your life off the stage so that your life on stage is stronger. The better we are as humans, the better we are as improvisers.

The pure art of improvisation in itself is incredible and we can never be 'finished'. We will never do the perfect show and even if we get close, we'll fall behind again. That is the trouble and the joy with improvisation and the fire for our addiction to it.

I hope to meet you someday if I haven't already – and I wish you the best of luck in your journey.

www.nickhernbooks.co.uk

facebook.com/nickhernbooks

twitter.com/nickhernbooks